# THE SECOND PRAYER-BOOK

## OF

## EDWARD VI.

### ISSUED 1552.

THIRD THOUSAND.

PUBLISHERS
Eugene, Oregon

Wipf and Stock Publishers
199 W 8th Ave, Suite 3
Eugene, OR 97401

The Second Prayer-Book of Edward VI, Issued 1552
By Parker, James
ISBN 13: 978-1-55635-051-1
ISBN: 1-55635-051-1
Publication date 11/6/2006
Previously published by Parker and Co., 1883

# EDITOR'S PREFACE.

IT has been thought well to issue, uniform with the one-shilling edition of Edward the Sixth's First Prayer-Book of 1549, an edition of the Second book of 1552.

The First book, though it was the work of staunch Reformers, including amongst others the names of Cranmer and Ridley, did not satisfy the cravings for novelty which some of the changes at the Reformation had engendered. Partly from political interests and supposed policy, partly from the circumstance that some of the Continental Reformers had taken refuge in England, the Prayer-Book was altered in the direction of conformity with the Calvinistic and Zuinglian services abroad by Peter Martyr, an Italian, and Martin Bucer, a German, without, so far as can be ascertained, any sanction of the Convocation being given to it; and this altered book, by the political party in power, was attached to an Act of Parliament.

The Bill was read the first time in the House of Lords on March 31, 1552, as "a Bill for a due Coming to Common Prayer and other Services of God in Churches on Sundays and other Holy Days." On April 6 it was sent down to the

Commons as a "Bill for the Uniformity of Service and Administration of the Sacraments to be had throughout the Realm, and therewithal a book of the said Service drawn out by certain Persons appointed by the King's Majesty for that purpose." It afterwards passed the Commons, and was returned to the House of Lords April 14 of the same year. As the session had commenced Jan. 23, and lasted till April 15, 1552, and as the regnal years of Edward VI. are reckoned from Jan. 28 [1547], this session of Parliament is known as that of the 5th and 6th of Edward VI.

The causes which led to the several changes made in the new book, or the principles on which the revisers proceeded, cannot be discussed here. The results will be seen by a patient reader who will be at the pains to compare the two books together.

As to the printing of this little volume, it may be said to be based upon an edition of Whitchurch of 1552; and as the same plan as to various readings, spelling, punctuation, and use of capitals adopted in printing the First Prayer-Book applies to this, there is no reason to repeat here what has been said in the preface to that volume.

JAMES PARKER.

*Nov.* 1882.

# THE BOOK OF COMMON PRAYER, AND ADMINISTRATION OF THE SACRAMENTS, AND OTHER RITES AND CEREMONIES IN THE CHURCH OF ENGLAND.

Londini in Officina
*Edvvardi Whitchurche.*
*Cum privilegio ad imprimendum solum.*
Anno 1552.

---

*Various Imprints.*

B Same as above (but a different book).
C Londini In Officina Richardi Graftoni Regii Impressoris. *Cum Privilegio ad Imprimendum solum. Anno 1552.*
D Ditto (but a different book).
E Ditto (but a different book).

# THE CONTENTS OF THIS BOOK.

i. A Preface.
ii. Of ceremonies, why some be abolished and some retained.
iii. The order how the Psalter is appointed to be read.
iv. The Table for the order of the Psalms to be said at Morning and Evening prayer.
v. The order how the rest of holy Scripture is appointed to be read.
vi. Proper Psalms and Lessons at Morning and Evening Prayer, for certain feasts and days.
vii. An Almanack.
viii. The Table and Kalendar for Psalms and Lessons, with necessary Rules appertaining to the same.
ix. The order for Morning Prayer and Evening Prayer throughout the year.
x. The Litany.
xi. The Collects, Epistles, and Gospels, to be used at the ministration of the holy Communion, throughout the year.
xii. The order of the ministration of the holy Communion.
xiii. Baptism both public and private.
xiv. Confirmation, where also is a Catechism for children.
xv. Matrimony.
xvi. Visitation of the sick.
xvii. The Communion of the sick.
xviii. Burial.
xix. The Thanksgiving of women after child-birth.
xx. A Commination against sinners, with certain prayers to be used divers times in the year.
xxi. The form and manner of making and consecrating of Bishops, Priests and Deacons.

# THE PREFACE.

[In several copies the Act of Uniformity is printed before this Preface.]

THERE was never any thing by the wit of man so well devised, or so sure established, which (in continuance of time) hath not been corrupted: as (among other things) it may plainly appear by the common prayers in the Church, commonly called divine service: the first original and ground whereof if a man would search out by the ancient fathers, he shall find that the same was not ordained but of a good purpose, and for a great advancement of godliness: For they so ordered the matter, that all the whole Bible (or the greatest part thereof) should be read over once in the year, intending thereby, that the Clergy, and specially such as were ministers of the congregation, should (by often reading and meditation of God's word) be stirred up to godliness themselves, and be more able also to exhort other by wholesome doctrine, and to confute them that were adversaries to the truth. And further, that the people (by daily hearing of holy scripture read in the Church) should continually profit more and more in the knowledge of God, and be the more inflamed with the love of his true religion. But these many years passed, this godly and decent order of the ancient fathers hath been so altered, broken, and neglected, by planting in uncertain stories, Legends, Responds, Verses, vain repetitions, Commemorations, and Synodals, that commonly when any book of the Bible was begun, before three or four chapters were read out, all the rest were unread. And in this sort the book of Esai was begun in Advent, and the book of Genesis in Septuagesima: but they were only begun, and never read through. After a like sort were other books of holy scripture used. And moreover, whereas Saint Paul would have such language spoken to the people in the church, as they might understand, and have profit by hearing the same: The service in this Church of England (these many years) hath been read in Latin to the people, which they understood not: so that they have heard with their ears only; and their hearts, spirit, and mind, have not been edified thereby. And furthermore, notwithstanding that the ancient fathers have divided the Psalms into seven portions, whereof every one was called a Nocturn; now of late time, a few of them have been daily said (and oft repeated) and the rest utterly omitted. Moreover, the number and hardness of the rules, called the Pie, and the manifold changings of the service, was the cause, that to turn the book only was so hard and intricate a matter, that many times there was more business to find out what should be read, than to read it when it was found out.

These inconveniences therefore considered, here is set forth such an order, whereby the same shall be redressed. And for a readiness in this matter, here is drawn out a kalendar for that purpose, which is plain and easy to be understanden: wherein (so much as may be) the reading of holy scriptures is so set forth, that all things shall be done in order, without breaking one piece thereof from another. For this cause be cut off Anthems, Responds, Invitatories, and such like things, as did break the continual course of the reading of the scripture. Yet because there is no remedy, but that of necessity there must be some rules, therefore certain rules are here set forth, which as they be few in number, so they be plain and easy to be understanden. So that here you have an order for prayer (as touching the reading of holy scripture) much agreeable to the mind and purpose of the old fathers, and a great deal more profitable and commodious, than that which of late was used. It is more profitable, because here are left out many things, whereof some be untrue, some uncertain, some vain and superstitious, and is ordained nothing to be read, but the very pure word of God, the holy scriptures, or that which is evidently grounded upon the same, and that in such a language and order, as is most easy and plain for the understanding, both of the readers and hearers. It is also more commodious, both for the shortness thereof, and for the plainness of the order, and for that the rules be few and easy. Furthermore, by this order, the curates shall need none other books for their public service, but this book, and the Bible: by the means whereof, the people shall not be at so great charge for books, as in time past they have been.

And where heretofore there hath been great diversity in saying and singing in Churches within this realm, some following Salisbury use, some Hereford use, some the use of Bangor, some of York, and some of Lincoln: Now from henceforth, all the whole realm shall have but one use. And if any would judge this way more painful, because that all things must be read upon the book, whereas before, by the reason of so often repetition, they could say many things by heart: if those men will weigh their labour, with the profit and knowledge, which daily they shall obtain by reading upon the book, they will not refuse the pain, in consideration of the great profit that shall ensue thereof.

And forasmuch as nothing can almost be so plainly set forth, but doubts may rise in the use and practising of the same: To appease all such diversity (if any arise), and for the resolution of all doubts, concerning the manner how to understand, do, and execute the things contained in this book: the parties that so doubt, or diversely take any thing, shall always resort to the Bishop of the Diocese, who by his discretion shall take order for the quieting and appeasing of the same: so that the same order be not contrary to any thing contained in this book. And if the Bishop of the Diocese be in any doubt, then may he send for resolution thereof unto the Archbishop.

Though it be appointed in the afore written Preface, that all things shall be read and sung in the Church, in the English tongue, to the end that the congregation may be thereby edified : yet it is not meant, but when men say Morning and Evening prayer privately, they may say the same in any language that they themselves do understand.

And all Priests and Deacons shall be bound to say daily the Morning and Evening prayer, either privately or openly, except they be letted by preaching, studying of divinity, or by some other urgent cause.

And the Curate that ministereth in every Parish Church or Chapel, being at home, and not being otherwise reasonably letted, shall say the same in the Parish Church or Chapel where he ministereth, and shall toll a bell thereto, a convenient time before he begin, that such as be disposed may come to hear God's word, and to pray with him.

## OF CEREMONIES,

#### WHY SOME BE ABOLISHED, AND SOME RETAINED.

Of such ceremonies as be used in the church, and have had their beginning by the institution of man: some at the first were of godly intent and purpose devised, and yet at length turned to vanity and superstition: some entered into the church by undiscreet devotion, and such a zeal as was without knowledge: and for because they were winked at in the beginning, they grew daily to more and more abuses: which not only for their unprofitableness, but also because they have much blinded the people, and obscured the glory of God, are worthy to be cut away, and clean rejected. Other there be, which although they have been devised by man, yet it is thought good to reserve them still, as well for a decent order in the church (for the which they were first devised) as because they pertain to edification: whereunto all things done in the church (as the Apostle teacheth) ought to be referred. And although the keeping or omitting of a ceremony (in itself considered) is but a small thing: yet the wilful and contemptuous transgression, and breaking of a common order and discipline, is no small offence before God.

Let all things be done among you (saith S. Paul) in a seemly and due order. The appointment of the which order pertaineth not to private men: therefore no man ought to take in hand, nor presume to appoint or alter any public or common order in Christ's church, except he be lawfully called and authorized thereunto.

And whereas in this our time, the minds of men are so diverse, that some think it a great matter of conscience to depart from a piece of the least of their ceremonies (they be so addicted to their old customs:) and again on the other side, some be so new fangled, that they would innovate all thing, and so do despise the old, that nothing can like them, but that is new: it was thought expedient, not so much to have respect how to please and satisfy either of these parties, as how to please God, and profit them both. And yet lest any man should be offended (whom good reason might satisfy) here be certain causes rendered why some of the accustomed ceremonies be put away, and some retained and kept still.

Some are put away, because the great excess and multitude of them hath so increased in these latter days, that the burden of them was intolerable: whereof S. Augustine in his time complained, that they were grown to such a number, that the state of Christian people was in worse case (concerning that matter) than were the Jews. And he counselled that such yoke and burden should be taken away, as time would serve quietly to do it.

But what would S. Augustine have said, if he had seen the ceremonies of late days used among us? whereunto the multitude used in his time was not to be compared. This our excessive multitude of Ceremonies was so great, and many of them so dark: that they did more confound, and darken, than declare and set forth Christ's benefits unto us.

And besides this, Christ's Gospel is not a Ceremonial law (as much of Moses' law was) but it is a religion to serve God, not in bondage of the figure or shadow, but in the freedom of spirit, being content only with those Ceremonies, which do serve to a decent order and godly discipline, and such as be apt to stir up the dull mind of man, to the remembrance of his duty to God, by some notable and special signification, whereby he might be edified.

Furthermore, the most weighty cause of the abolishment of certain Ceremonies was, that they were so far abused, partly by the superstitious blindness of the rude and unlearned, and partly by the unsatiable avarice of such as sought more their own lucre, than the glory of God; that the abuses could not well be taken away, the thing remaining still. But now as concerning those persons, which peradventure will be offended, for that some of the old ceremonies are retained still: if they consider, that without some ceremonies it is not possible to keep any order or quiet discipline in the church, they shall easily perceive just cause to reform their judgments. And if they think much that any of the old do remain, and would rather have all devised anew: Then such men (granting some ceremonies convenient to be had), surely where the old may be well used, there they cannot reasonably reprove the old only for their age without bewraying of their own folly. For in such a case, they ought rather to have reverence unto them for their antiquity, if they will declare themselves to be more studious of unity and concord, than of innovations and newfangleness, which (as much as may be with the true setting forth of Christ's Religion) is always to be eschewed. Furthermore, such shall have no just cause with the ceremonies reserved to be offended: For as those be taken away, which were most abused, and did burden men's consciences without any cause: so the other that remain are retained for a Discipline and order, which (upon just causes) may be altered and changed, and therefore are not to be esteemed equal with God's law. And moreover they be neither dark nor dumb ceremonies: but are so set forth, that every man may understand what they do mean, and to what use they do serve. So that it is not like that they in time to come, should be abused as the other have been. And in these our doings, we condemn no other nations, nor prescribe any thing, but to our own people only. For we think it convenient that every country should use such ceremonies, as they shall think best to the setting forth of God's honour or glory, and to the reducing of the people to a most perfect and godly living, without error or superstition. And that they should put away other things, which from time to time they perceive to be most abused, as in men's ordinances it often chanceth diversely in diverse countries.

## THE TABLE AND KALENDAR

EXPRESSING THE ORDER OF THE PSALMS AND LESSONS, TO BE SAID AT THE MORNING AND EVENING PRAYER THROUGHOUT THE YEAR, EXCEPT CERTAIN PROPER FEASTS, AS THE RULES FOLLOWING MORE PLAINLY DECLARE.

**THE ORDER HOW THE PSALTER IS APPOINTED TO BE READ.**

THE Psalter shall be read through once every Month. And because that some Months be longer than some other be, it is thought good to make them even by this means.

To every Month shall be appointed (as concerning this purpose) just xxx days.

And because January and March hath one day above the said number, and February which is placed between them both, hath only xxviii days: February shall borrow of either of the months (of January and March) one day. And so the Psalter which shall be read in February, must begin the last day of January, and end the first day of March.

And whereas May, July, August, October and December, have xxxi days apiece, it is ordered that the same Psalms shall be read the last day of the said

Months, which were read the day before. So that the Psalter may begin again the first day of the next Months ensuing.

Now to know what Psalms shall be read every day, look in the Kalendar the number that is appointed for the Psalms, and then find the same number in this table, and upon that number shall you see, what Psalms shall be said at Morning and Evening Prayer.

And where the cxix Psalm is divided into xxii portions, and is over long to be read at one time: it is so ordered, that at one time shall not be read above four or five of the said portions, as you shall perceive to be noted in this Table following.

And here is also to be noted, that in this table, and in all other parts of the service, where any Psalms are appointed, the number is expressed after the great English Bible, which from the ix Psalm unto the cxlviiith Psalm (following the division of the Hebrues) doth vary in numbers from the common Latin translation.

# THE TABLE

## For the Order of the Psalms, to be said at Morning and Evening Prayer.

|        | ℭ Morning Prayer.            | ℭ Evening Prayer.              |
|--------|------------------------------|--------------------------------|
| i.     | i, ii, iii, iv, v.           | vi, vii, viii.                 |
| ii.    | ix, x, xi.                   | xii, xiii, xiv.                |
| iii.   | xv, xvi, xvii.               | xviii.                         |
| iv.    | xix, xx, xxi                 | xxii, xxiii.                   |
| v.     | xxiv, xxv, xxvi.             | xxvii, xxviii, xxix.           |
| vi.    | xxx, xxxi.                   | xxxii, xxxiii, xxxiv.          |
| vii.   | xxxv, xxxvi.                 | xxxvii.                        |
| viii.  | xxxviii, xxxix, xl.          | xli, xlii, xliii.              |
| ix.    | xliv, xlv, xlvi.             | xlvii, xlviii, xlix.           |
| x.     | l, li, lii.                  | liii, liv, lv.                 |
| xi.    | lvi, lvii, lviii.            | lix, lx, lxi.                  |
| xii.   | lxii, lxiii, lxiv.           | lxv, lxvi, lxvii.              |
| xiii.  | lxviii.                      | lxix, lxx.                     |
| xiv.   | lxxi, lxxii.                 | lxxiii, lxxiv.                 |
| xv.    | lxxv, lxxvi, lxxvii.         | lxxviii.                       |
| xvi.   | lxxix, lxxx, lxxxi.          | lxxxii, lxxxiii, lxxxiv, lxxxv. |
| xvii.  | lxxxvi, lxxxvii, lxxxviii.   | lxxxix.                        |
| xviii. | xc, xci, xcii.               | xciii, xciv.                   |
| xix.   | xcvi, xcvii.                 | xcviii, xcix, c, ci.           |
| xx.    | cii, ciii.                   | civ.                           |
| xxi.   | cv.                          | cvi.                           |
| xxii.  | cvii.                        | cviii, cix.                    |
| xxiii. | cx, cxi, cxii, cxiii.        | cxiv, cxv.                     |
| xxiv.  | cxvi, cxvii, cxviii.         | cxix. Inde. iv.                |
| xxv.   | Inde. v.                     | Inde. iv.                      |
| xxvi.  | Inde. v.                     | Inde. iv.                      |
| xxvii. | cxx, cxxi, cxxii, cxxiii, cxxiv, cxxv. | cxxvi, cxxvii, cxxviii, cxxix, cxxx, cxxxi. |
| xxviii.| cxxxii, cxxxiii, cxxxiv, cxxxv. | cxxxvi, cxxxvii, cxxxviii.  |
| xxix.  | cxxxix, cxl, cxli.           | cxlii, cxliii.                 |
| xxx.   | cxliv, cxlv, cxlvi.          | cxlvii, cxlviii, cxlix, cl.    |

# THE ORDER

## HOW THE REST OF HOLY SCRIPTURE (BESIDE THE PSALTER) IS APPOINTED TO BE READ.

The Old Testament is appointed for the first Lessons, at Morning and Evening prayer, and shall be read through every year once, except certain books and chapters, which be least edifying, and might best be spared, and therefore be left unread.

The New Testament is appointed for the second Lessons, at Morning and Evening prayer, and shall be read over orderly every year thrice, beside the Epistles and Gospels: except the Apocalypse, out of the which there be only certain Lessons appointed, upon divers proper feasts.

And to know what Lessons shall be read every day: find the day of the month in the Kalendar following: and there ye shall perceive the books and Chapters, that shall be read for the Lessons, both at Morning and Evening prayer.

And here is to be noted, that whensoever there be any proper Psalms or Lessons appointed for any feast, moveable or unmoveable: then the Psalms and Lessons appointed in the Kalendar, shall be omitted for that time.

Ye must note also, that the Collect, Epistle, and Gospel, appointed for the Sunday, shall serve all the week after, except there fall some feast that hath his proper.

This is also to be noted, concerning the leap years, that the xxvth day of February, which in leap year is counted for two days, shall in those two days alter neither Psalm nor Lesson: but the same Psalms and Lessons, which be said the first day, shall also serve for the second day.

Also, wheresoever the beginning of any Lesson, Epistle, or Gospel is not expressed: there ye must begin at the beginning of the Chapter.

And wheresoever is not expressed how far shall be read, there shall you read to the end of the Chapter.

# PROPER PSALMS AND LESSONS FOR DIVERS FEASTS AND DAYS,

## AT MORNING AND EVENING PRAYER.

On Christmas day at Morning prayer.
- Psalm xix.
- Psalm xlv.
- Psalm lxxxv.

The first Lesson. Esay. ix.
The ii. Lesson. Luk. ii. *unto* And unto men a good will.

At Evening prayer.
- Psalm lxxxix.
- Psalm cx.
- Psalm cxxxii.

The first Lesson. Esa. vii. God spake once again to Achas. &c., *unto the end*.
The second Lesson. Tit. iii. The kindness and love. &c. *unto* foolish questions.

On Saint Stephen's day, at Morning prayer.
The second Lesson. Acts vi. and vii. Stephen full of faith and power, *unto* And when forty years were. &c.

At Evening prayer.
The second Lesson. Acts vii. And when forty years were expired, there appeared unto Moses. &c. *unto* Stephen full of the Holy Ghost.

On Saint John the Evangelist's day, at Morning prayer.
The second Lesson. Apoca. i. The whole Chapter.

At Evening prayer.
The second Lesson. Apocalips. xxii.

On the Innocents' day, at Morning prayer.
The first Lesson. Jerem. xxxi. *unto* Moreover I heard Ephraim.

## PROPER PSALMS AND LESSONS, &c.

On the Circumcision day, at Morning prayer.
- The first Lesson. Genesis. xvii.
- The second Lesson. Roma. ii.

At Evening prayer.
- The first Lesson. Deut. x. And now Israel. &c.
- The second Lesson. Colos. ii.

On the Epiphany, at Morning Prayer.
- The first Lesson. Esay. lx.
- The second Lesson. Luke iii. And it fortuned, &c.

At Evening prayer.
- The first Lesson. Esay. xlix.
- The second Lesson. John ii. After this he went down to Capernaum.

On Wednesday before Easter, at Evening prayer.
- The first Lesson. Ozee. xiii. xiv.

On Thursday before Easter, at Morning prayer.
- The first Lesson. Daniel. ix.

At Evening prayer.
- The first Lesson. Jeremie. xxxi.

On Good Friday, at Morning prayer.
- The first Lesson. Genesis. xxii.

At Evening prayer.
- The first Lesson. Esay. liii.

On Easter Even, at Morning prayer.
- The first Lesson. Zachary. ix.

On Easter day, at Morning prayer.
- Psalm ii.
- Psalm lvii.
- Psalm cxi.
- The first Lesson. Exodi. xii.
- The second Lesson. Ro. vi.

| | | |
|---|---|---|
| At Evening prayer. | Psalm cxiii.<br>Psalm cxiv.<br>Psalm cxviii. | The second Lesson. Act. ii. |
| On Monday in Easter week, at Morning prayer. | | The second Lesson. Math. xxviii. |
| At Evening prayer. | | The second Lesson. Acts. iii. |
| On Tuesday in Easter week, at Morning prayer. | | The second Lesson. Luke xxiv. *unto* And behold two of them. |
| At Evening prayer. | | The second Lesson. 1 Corin. xv. |
| On the Ascension day, at Morning prayer. | Psalm viii.<br>Psalm xv.<br>Psalm xxi. | The ii. Lesson. John. xiv. |
| At Evening prayer. | Psalm xxiv.<br>Psalm lxviii.<br>Psalm cviii. | The ii. Lesson. Ephe. iv. |
| On Whitsunday, at Morning prayer. | Psalm xlviii.<br>Psalm lxvii. | The second Lesson. Act. x. Then Peter opened his, &c. |
| At Evening prayer. | Psalm civ.<br>Psalm cxlv. | The second Lesson. Act. xix. It fortuned when Apollo went to Corinthum, &c. *unto* After these things. |
| On Trinity Sunday, at Morning prayer. | | The first Lesson. Gene. xviii.<br>The second Lesson. Math. iii. |

## PROPER PSALMS AND LESSONS, &c. 19

| | |
|---|---|
| Conversion of Saint Paul, at Morning prayer. | The second Lesson. Acts. xxii. *unto* They heard him. |
| At Evening prayer. | The second Lesson. Acts. xxvi. |
| Saint Barnabie's day, at Morning prayer. | The second Lesson. Acts. xiv. |
| At Evening prayer. | The second Lesson. Acts. xv. *unto* After certain days. |
| St. John Baptist's day, at Morning prayer. | The first Lesson. Malachi. iii.<br>The second Lesson. Math. iii. |
| At Evening prayer. | The first Lesson. Malachi. iv.<br>The second Lesson. Math. xiv. *unto* When Jesus heard. |
| Saint Peter's day, at Morning prayer. | The second Lesson. Acts. iii. |
| At Evening prayer. | The second Lesson. Acts. iv. |
| All Saints' day at Morning prayer. | The first Lesson. Sapien. iii. *unto* Blessed is rather the barren.<br>The second Lesson. Hebrew xi. xii. Saints by faith subdued. *unto* If you endure chastising. |
| At Evening prayer. | The first Lesson. Sapience. v. *unto* His jealousy also.<br>The second Lesson. Apocalyps xix. *unto* And I saw an angel stand. |

# AN ALMANACK FOR NINETEEN YEARS.

| The year of our Lord. | The Golden Number. | The epact. | The Cycle of the sun. | Dominical letter. | Easter day. |
|---|---|---|---|---|---|
| 1552 | xiv | iv | xxi | C. B. | xvii April. |
| 1553 | xv | xv | xxii | A. | ii April. |
| 1554 | xvi | xxvi | xxiii | G. | xxv March. |
| 1555 | xvii | vii | xxiv | F. | xiv April. |
| 1556 | xviii | xviii | xxv | E. D. | v April. |
| 1557 | xix | xxix | xxvi | C. | xviii April. |
| 1558 | i | xi | xxvii | B. | x April. |
| 1559 | ii | xxii | xxviii | A. | xxvi March. |
| 1560 | iii | iii | i | G. F. | xiv April. |
| 1561 | iv | xiv | ii | E. | vi April. |
| 1562 | v | xxv | iii | D. | [a] [22 Mar. |
| 1563 | vi | xxvi | iv | C. | 11 April. |
| 1564 | vii | xvii | v | B. A. | 3 April. |
| 1565 | viii | xxviii | vi | G. | 22 April. |
| 1566 | ix | ix | vii | F. | 7 April. |
| 1567 | x | xx | viii | E. | 30 Mar. |
| 1568 | xi | i | ix | D. C. | 8 Mar. |
| 1569 | xii | xii | x | B. | 10 Ap. |
| 1570 | xiii | xxiii | xi | A. | 26 Mar.] |

[a] This continuation (with four errors in nine dates) appears only in one ed., 1552. The other editions leave the column blank.

## JANUARY HATH XXXI. DAYS.

|   |   |   | *Psalms.* | MORNING PRAYER. | | EVENING PRAYER. | |
|---|---|---|---|---|---|---|---|
|   |   |   |   | 1 *Lesson.* | 2 *Lesson.* | 1 *Lesson.* | 2 *Lesson.* |
| A | *Kalend.* | Circumci- | 1 | Gen. 17 | Roma. 2 | Deut. 10 | Collos. 2 |
| b | 4 No. | [sion. | 2 | Genesis 1 | Math. 1 | Gene. 2 | Roman 1 |
| c | 3 No. |   | 3 | 3 | 2 | 4 | 2 |
| d | Prid. No. |   | 4 | 5 | 3 | 6 | 3 |
| e | *Nonas.* |   | 5 | 7 | 4 | 8 | 4 |
| f | 8 Id. | Epiphanie. | 6 | Esai. 60 | Luke 3 | Esai. 49 | Jhon 2 |
| g | 7 Id. |   | 7 | Genesi 9 | Math. 5 | Genesi 11 | Roma. 5 |
| A | 6 Id. |   | 8 | 12 | 6 | 13 | 6 |
| b | 5 Id. |   | 9 | 14 | 7 | 15 | 7 |
| c | 4 Id. |   | 10 | 16 | 8 | 17 | 8 |
| d | 3 Id. |   | 11 | 18 | 9 | 19 | 9 |
| e | Prid. Id. | Sol in | 12 | 20 | 10 | 21 | 10 |
| f | *Idus.* | [aqua. | 13 | 22 | 11 | 23 | 11 |
| g | 19 kl. | Februarii. | 14 | 24 | 12 | 25 | 12 |
| A | 18 kl. |   | 15 | 26 | 13 | 27 | 13 |
| b | 17 kl. | Term be- | 16 | 28 | 14 | 29 | 14 |
| c | 16 kl. | [gin. | 17 | 30 | 15 | 31 | 15 |
| d | 15 kl. |   | 18 | 32 | 16 | 33 | 16 |
| e | 14 kl. |   | 19 | 34 | 17 | 35 | 1 Corin. 1 |
| f | 13 kl. |   | 20 | 36 | 18 | 37 | 2 |
| g | 12 kl. |   | 21 | 39 | 19 | 39 | 3 |
| A | 11 kl. |   | 22 | 40 | 20 | 41 | 4 |
| b | 10 kl. |   | 23 | 42 | 21 | 43 | 5 |
| c | 9 kl. |   | 24 | 44 | 22 | 45 | 6 |
| d | 8 kl. | Con. Pauls | 25 | 46 | Act. 22 | 47 | Acte. 26 |
| e | 7 kl. |   | 26 | 48 | Mat. 23 | 49 | 1 Cor. 7 |
| f | 6 kl. |   | 27 | 50 | 24 | Exod. 1 | 8 |
| g | 5 kl. |   | 28 | Exodi 2 | 25 | 3 | 9 |
| A | 4 kl. |   | 29 | 4 | 26 | 5 | 10 |
| b | 3 kl. |   | 30 | 6 | 27 | 7 | 11 |
| c | Prid. kl. |   | 1 | 8 | 28 | 9 | 12 |

## FEBRUARY HATH XXVIII. DAYS.

| | | | | Psalms. | MORNING PRAYER. | | EVENING PRAYER. | |
|---|---|---|---|---|---|---|---|---|
| | | | | | 1 Lesson. | 2 Lesson. | 1 Lesson. | 2 Lesson. |
|    | d | *Kalend.* |            | 2  | Exod. 10 | Marke 1 | Exod. 11 | 1 Cor. 13 |
| 11 | e | 4 No.     | *Pur. Mary*| 3  | 12       | 2       | 13       | 14 |
| 19 | f | 3 No.     |            | 4  | 14       | 3       | 15       | 15 |
| 8  | g | Prid. No. |            | 5  | 16       | 4       | 17       | 16 |
|    | A | *Nonas.*  |            | 6  | 18       | 5       | 19       | 2 Corin. 1 |
| 16 | b | 8 Id.     |            | 7  | 20       | 6       | 21       | 2 |
| 5  | c | 7 Id.     |            | 8  | 22       | 7       | 23       | 3 |
|    | d | 6 Id.     |            | 9  | 24       | 8       | 32       | 4 |
| 13 | e | 5 Id.     |            | 10 | 33       | 9       | 34       | 5 |
| 2  | f | 4 Id.     | *Sol in pisc.* | 11 | 35   | 10      | 40       | 6 |
|    | g | 3 Id.     |            | 12 | Lev. 18  | 11      | Lev. 19  | 7 |
| 10 | A | Prid. Id. |            | 13 | 20       | 12      | Nume. 10 | 8 |
|    | b | *Idus.*   |            | 14 | Nume 11  | 13      | 12       | 9 |
| 18 | c | 16 kl.    | March.     | 15 | 13       | 14      | 14       | 10 |
| 7  | d | 15 kl.    |            | 16 | 15       | 15      | 16       | 11 |
|    | e | 14 kl.    |            | 17 | 17       | 16      | 18       | 12 |
| 15 | f | 13 kl.    |            | 18 | 19       | Luk. di. 1 | 20    | 13 |
| 4  | g | 12 kl.    |            | 19 | 21       | di. 1   | 22       | Galath. 1 |
|    | A | 11 kl.    |            | 20 | 23       | 2       | 24       | 2 |
| 12 | b | 10 kl.    |            | 21 | 25       | 3       | 26       | 3 |
| 1  | c | 9 kl.     |            | 22 | 27       | 4       | 28       | 4 |
|    | d | 8 kl.     |            | 23 | 29       | 5       | 30       | 5 |
| 9  | e | 7 kl.     |            | 24 | 31       | 6       | 32       | 6 |
|    | f | 6 kl.     | *S. Mat-*  | 25 | 33       | 7       | 34       | Ephesi. 1 |
| 17 | g | 5 kl.     | [*thias.*  | 26 | 35       | 8       | 36       | 2 |
| 6  | A | 4 kl.     |            | 27 | Deut. 1  | 9       | Deut. 2  | 3 |
|    | b | 3 kl.     |            | 28 | 3        | 10      | 4        | 4 |
| 14 | c | *Prid.* kl.|           | 29 | 5        | 11      | 6        | 5 |

## MARCH HATH XXXI. DAYS.

|     |   |          |              | Psalms. | MORNING PRAYER. |           | EVENING PRAYER. |          |
|-----|---|----------|--------------|---------|-----------------|-----------|-----------------|----------|
|     |   |          |              |         | 1 *Lesson.*     | 2 *Lesson.* | 1 *Lesson.*   | 2 *Lesson.* |
| 3   | d | *Kalend.* |              | 30      | Deut. 7         | Luke 12   | Deut. 8         | Ephe. 6  |
|     | e | 6 No.    |              | 1       | 9               | 13        | 10              | Philip. 1 |
| 11  | f | 5 No.    |              | 2       | 11              | 14        | 12              | 2        |
|     | g | 4 No.    |              | 3       | 13              | 15        | 14              | 3        |
| 19  | A | 3 No.    |              | 4       | 15              | 16        | 16              | 4        |
| 8   | b | Prid. No. |             | 5       | 17              | 17        | 18              | Collo. 1 |
|     | c | *Nonas.* |              | 6       | 19              | 18        | 20              | 2        |
| 16  | d | 8 Id.    |              | 7       | 21              | 19        | 22              | 3        |
| 5   | e | 7 Id.    |              | 8       | 23              | 20        | 24              | 4        |
|     | f | 6 Id.    |              | 9       | 25              | 21        | 26              | 1 Thes. 1 |
| 13  | g | 5 Id.    | Equinoctiũ   | 10      | 27              | 22        | 28              | 2        |
| 2   | A | 4 Id.    | Sol in       | 11      | 29              | 23        | 30              | 3        |
|     | b | 3 Id.    | [ariete.     | 12      | 31              | 24        | 32              | 4        |
| 10  | c | Prid. Id. |             | 13      | 33              | Jhon. 1   | 34              | 5        |
|     | d | *Idus.*  |              | 14      | Josue. 1        | 2         | Josue. 2        | 2 Thes. 1 |
| 18  | e | 17 kL    | Aprilis.     | 15      | 3               | 3         | 3               | 2        |
| 7   | f | 16 kL    |              | 16      | 4               | 4         | 4               | 3        |
|     | g | 15 kL    |              | 17      | 5               | 5         | 5               | 1 Timo. 1 |
| 15  | A | 14 kl.   |              | 18      | 6               | 6         | 6               | 2. 3     |
| 4   | b | 13 kl.   |              | 19      | 7               | 7         | 7               | 4        |
|     | c | 12 kl.   |              | 20      | 8               | 8         | 8               | 5        |
| 12  | d | 11 kl.   |              | 21      | 9               | 9         | 9               | 6        |
| 1   | e | 10 kl.   |              | 22      | 10              | 10        | 11              | 2 Tim. 1 |
|     | f | 9 kl.    |              | 23      | 12              | 11        | 20              | 2        |
| 9   | g | 8 kl.    | Annuncia-    | 24      | 21              | 12        | 22              | 3        |
|     | A | 7 kl.    | [cio.        | 25      | 23              | 13        | 24              | 4        |
| 17  | b | 6 kl.    |              | 26      | Judic. 1        | 14        | Judic. 2        | Titus 1  |
| 6   | c | 5 kl.    |              | 27      | 3               | 15        | 4               | 2. 3     |
|     | d | 4 kl.    |              | 28      | 5               | 16        | 6               | Phile. 1 |
| 14  | e | 3 kl.    |              | 29      | 7               | 17        | 8               | Hebreo.1 |
| 3   | f | *Prid.* kl. |           | 30      | 9               | 18        | 10              | 2        |

## APRIL HATH XXX. DAYS.

|  |  |  | | *Psalms.* | MORNING PRAYER. | | EVENING PRAYER. | |
|---|---|---|---|---|---|---|---|---|
|  |  |  |  |  | 1 Lesson. | 2 Lesson. | 1 Lesson. | 2 Lesson. |
|    | g | Kalend.       |              | 1  | Judic. 11 | Jhon 19 | Judi. 12 | Hebre. 3 |
| 11 | A | 4 No.         |              | 2  | 13        | 20      | 14       | 4 |
|    | b | 3 No.         |              | 3  | 15        | 21      | 16       | 5 |
| 19 | c | Prid. No.     |              | 4  | 17        | Acts 1  | 18       | 6 |
| 8  | d | Nonas.        |              | 5  | 19        | 2       | 20       | 7 |
| 16 | e | 8 Id.         |              | 6  | 21        | 3       | Ruth 1   | 8 |
| 5  | f | 7 Id.         |              | 7  | Ruth 2    | 4       | 3        | 9 |
|    | g | 6 Id.         |              | 8  | 4         | 5       | 1 Reg. 1 | 10 |
| 13 | A | 5 Id.         |              | 9  | 1 Regū. 2 | 6       | 3        | 11 |
| 2  | b | 4 Id.         |              | 10 | 4         | 7       | 5        | 12 |
|    | c | 3 Id.         |              | 11 | 6         | 8       | 7        | 13 |
| 10 | d | Prid. Id.     | *Sol in tau.*| 12 | 8         | 9       | 9        | Jacob. 1 |
|    | e | Idus.         |              | 13 | 10        | 10      | 11       | 2 |
| 18 | f | 18 kl.        | Maii.        | 14 | 12        | 11      | 13       | 3 |
| 7  | g | 17 kl.        |              | 15 | 14        | 12      | 15       | 4 |
|    | A | 16 kl.        |              | 16 | 16        | 13      | 17       | 5 |
| 15 | b | 15 kl.        |              | 17 | 18        | 14      | 19       | 1 Petr. 1 |
| 4  | c | 14 kl.        |              | 18 | 20        | 15      | 21       | 2 |
|    | d | 13 kl.        |              | 19 | 22        | 16      | 23       | 3 |
| 12 | e | 12 kl.        |              | 20 | 24        | 17      | 25       | 4 |
| 1  | f | 11 kl.        |              | 21 | 26        | 18      | 27       | 5 |
|    | g | 10 kl.        |              | 22 | 28        | 19      | 29       | 2 Petr. 1 |
| 9  | A | 9 kl.         | S. George.   | 23 | 30        | 20      | 31       | 2 |
|    | b | 8 kl.         |              | 24 | 2 Regū. 1 | 21      | 2 Re. 2  | 3 |
| 17 | c | 7 kl.         | MarkEva.     | 25 | 3         | 22      | 4        | 1 Jhon. 1 |
| 6  | d | 6 kl.         |              | 26 | 5         | 23      | 6        | 2 |
|    | e | 5 kl.         |              | 27 | 7         | 24      | 8        | 3 |
| 14 | f | 4 kl.         |              | 28 | 9         | 25      | 10       | 4 |
| 3  | g | 3 kl.         |              | 29 | 11        | 26      | 12       | 5 |
|    | A | Prid. kl.     |              | 30 | 13        | 27      | 14       | 2. 3. Jhō. |

## MAY HATH XXXI. DAYS.

|    |   |          |            | Psalms. | MORNING PRAYER. | | EVENING PRAYER. | |
|----|---|----------|------------|---------|-----------|-----------|-----------|-----------|
|    |   |          |            |         | 1 *Lesson.* | 2 *Lesson.* | 1 *Lesson.* | 2 *Lesson.* |
| 11 | b | *Kalend.* | Philip &   | 1       | 2 Reg. 15 | Acte 8    | 2 re. 16  | Judas. 1  |
|    | c | 6 No.    | Jac.       | 2       | 17        | 28        | 18        | Roma. 1   |
| 19 | d | 5 No.    |            | 3       | 19        | Matth. 1  | 20        | 2         |
| 8  | e | 4 No.    |            | 4       | 21        | 2         | 22        | 3         |
|    | f | 3 No.    |            | 5       | 23        | 3         | 24        | 4         |
| 16 | g | Prid. No.|            | 6       | 3 Regū. 1 | 4         | 3 Re. 2   | 5         |
| 5  | A | *Nonas.* |            | 7       | 3         | 5         | 4         | 6         |
|    | b | 8 Id.    |            | 8       | 5         | 6         | 6         | 7         |
| 13 | c | 7 Id.    |            | 9       | 7         | 7         | 8         | 8         |
| 2  | d | 6 Id.    |            | 10      | 9         | 8         | 10        | 9         |
|    | e | 5 Id.    | *Sol in gem.* | 11   | 11        | 9         | 12        | 10        |
| 10 | f | 4 Id.    |            | 12      | 13        | 10        | 14        | 11        |
|    | g | 3 Id.    |            | 13      | 15        | 11        | 16        | 12        |
| 18 | A | Prid. Id.|            | 14      | 17        | 12        | 18        | 13        |
| 7  | b | *Idus.*  |            | 15      | 19        | 13        | 20        | 14        |
|    | c | 17 kl.   | Junii.     | 16      | 21        | 14        | 22        | 15        |
| 15 | d | 16 kl.   |            | 17      | 4 Reg. 1  | 15        | 4 re. 2   | 16        |
| 4  | e | 15 kl.   |            | 18      | 3         | 16        | 4         | 1 Corin. 1|
|    | f | 14 kl.   |            | 19      | 5         | 17        | 6         | 2         |
| 12 | g | 13 kl.   |            | 20      | 7         | 18        | 8         | 3         |
| 1  | A | 12 kl.   |            | 21      | 9         | 19        | 10        | 4         |
|    | b | 11 kl.   |            | 22      | 11        | 20        | 12        | 5         |
| 9  | c | 10 kl.   |            | 23      | 13        | 21        | 14        | 6         |
|    | d | 9 kl.    |            | 24      | 15        | 22        | 16        | 7         |
| 17 | e | 8 kl.    |            | 25      | 17        | 23        | 18        | 8         |
| 6  | f | 7 kl.    |            | 26      | 19        | 24        | 20        | 9         |
|    | g | 6 kl.    |            | 27      | 21        | 25        | 22        | 10        |
| 14 | A | 5 kl.    |            | 28      | 23        | 26        | 24        | 11        |
| 3  | b | 4 kl.    |            | 29      | 25        | 27        | 25        | 12        |
|    | c | 3 kl.    |            | 30      | 1 Esdra 1 | 28        | 1 Esd. 2  | 13        |
| 11 | d | Prid. kl.|            | 30      | 3         | Marke 1   | 4         | 14        |

## JUNE HATH XXX. DAYS.

|    |   |           |             | Psalms. | MORNING PRAYER. | | EVENING PRAYER. | |
|----|---|-----------|-------------|----|----------|----------|----------|----------|
|    |   |           |             |    | 1 *Lesson.* | 2 *Lesson.* | 1 *Lesson.* | 2 *Lesson.* |
|    | e | *Kalend.* |             | 1  | 1 Esd. 4 | Mark 2   | 1 Esd. 5 | 1 Cor. 15 |
| 19 | f | 4 No.     |             | 2  | 6        | 3        | 6        | 16 |
| 8  | g | 3 No.     |             | 3  | 7        | 4        | 7        | 2 Corin. 1 |
| 15 | A | Prid. No. |             | 4  | 8        | 5        | 8        | 2 |
| 5  | b | *Nonas.*  |             | 5  | 9        | 6        | 10       | 3 |
|    | c | 8 Id.     |             | 6  | 2 Esdra 1 | 7       | 3        | 4 |
| 4  | d | 7 Id.     |             | 7  | 4        | 8        | 5        | 5 |
| 2  | e | 6 Id.     |             | 8  | 6        | 9        | 8        | 6 |
|    | f | 5 Id.     |             | 9  | 9        | 10       | 13       | 7 |
| 10 | g | 4 Id.     |             | 10 | Hester 1 | 11       | Hest. 2  | 8 |
|  . | A | 3 Id.     |             | 11 | 3        | Acte 14  | 4        | Actes 15 |
| 18 | b | Prid. Id. |             | 12 | 5        | Mark 12  | 6        | 2 Cor. 9 |
| 7  | c | *Idus.*   | Sol in Can. | 13 | 7        | 13       | 8        | 10 |
|    | d | 18 kl.    | Julii.      | 14 | 9        | 14       | Job 1    | 11 |
| 15 | e | 17 kl.    |             | 15 | Job. 2   | 15       | 3        | 12 |
| 4  | f | 16 kl.    |             | 16 | 4        | 16       | 5        | 13 |
|    | g | 15 kl.    | Term be-    | 17 | 6        | Luke 1   | 7        | Galath. 1 |
| 12 | A | 14 kl.    | [gin.       | 18 | 8        | 2        | 9        | 2 |
| 1  | b | 13 kl.    |             | 19 | 10       | 3        | 11       | 3 |
|    | c | 12 kl.    |             | 20 | 12       | 4        | 13       | 4 |
| 9  | d | 11 kl.    |             | 21 | 14       | 5        | 15       | 5 |
|    | e | 10 kl.    |             | 22 | 16       | 6        | 17. 18   | 6 |
| 17 | f | 9 kl.     |             | 23 | 19       | 7        | 20       | Ephesi. 1 |
| 6  | g | 8 kl.     | *Jhon bap-* | 24 | Mala. 3  | Matth. 3 | Mal. 3   | Mat. 14 |
|    | A | 7 kl.     | [tist.      | 25 | Job 21   | Luke 8   | Job 22   | Ephe. 2 |
| 14 | b | 6 kl.     |             | 26 | 23       | 9        | 24. 25   | 3 |
| 3  | c | 5 kl.     |             | 27 | 26. 27   | 10       | 28       | 4 |
|    | d | 4 kl.     |             | 28 | 29       | 11       | 30       | 5 |
| 11 | e | 3 kl.     | *S. Peter*  | 29 | 31       | Actes 3  | 32       | Actes 4 |
|    | f | Prid. kl. | [*ap.*      | 30 | 33       | Luke 12  | 34       | Ephes. 6 |

# SECOND PRAYER-BOOK OF EDWARD VI. 1552.

## JULY HATH XXXI. DAYS.

| | | | | *Psalms.* | MORNING PRAYER. | | EVENING PRAYER. | |
|---|---|---|---|---|---|---|---|---|
| | | | | | 1 *Lesson.* | 2 *Lesson.* | 1 *Lesson.* | 2 *Lesson.* |
| 19 | g | *Kalend.* | | 1 | Job 35 | Luk. 13 | Job 36 | Philip. 1 |
| 8 | A | 6 No. | | 2 | 37 | 14 | 38 | 2 |
| | b | 5 No. | | 3 | 39 | 15 | 40 | 3 |
| 16 | c | 4 No. | | 4 | 41 | 16 | 42 | 4 |
| 5 | d | 3 No. | [*ende.* | 5 | Prover. 1 | 17 | Prov. 2 | Collos. 1 |
| | e | Prid. No. | *Terme* | 6 | 3 | 18 | 4 | 2 |
| 13 | f | *Nonas.* | Dog daies. | 7 | 5 | 19 | 6 | 3 |
| 2 | g | 8 Id. | | 8 | 7 | 20 | 8 | 4 |
| | A | 7 Id. | | 9 | 9 | 21 | 10 | 1 Tessa. 1 |
| 10 | b | 6 Id. | | 10 | 11 | 22 | 12 | 2 |
| | c | 5 Id. | | 11 | 13 | 23 | 14 | 3 |
| 18 | d | 4 Id. | | 12 | 15 | 24 | 16 | 4 |
| 7 | e | 3 Id. | | 13 | 17 | Ihon 1 | 18 | 5 |
| | f | Prid. Id. | *Sol in Leo.* | 14 | 19 | 2 | 20 | 2 Thess. 1 |
| 15 | g | *Idus.* | | 15 | 21 | 3 | 22 | 2 |
| 4 | A | 17 kl. | Augusti. | 16 | 23 | 4 | 24 | 3 |
| | b | 16 kl. | | 17 | 25 | 5 | 26 | 1 Timo. 1 |
| 12 | c | 15 kl. | | 18 | 27 | 6 | 28 | 2, 3 |
| 1 | d | 14 kl. | | 19 | 29 | 7 | 30 | 4 |
| | e | 13 kl. | | 20 | 31 | 8 | Eccle. 1 | 5 |
| 9 | f | 12 kl. | | 21 | Eccles. 2 | 9 | 3 | 6 |
| | g | 11 kl. | | 22 | 4 | 10 | 5 | 2 Tim. 1 |
| 17 | A | 10 kl. | | 23 | 6 | 11 | 7 | 2 |
| 6 | b | 9 kl. | | 24 | 8 | 12 | 9 | 3 |
| | c | 8 kl. | *James Apo* | 25 | 10 | 13 | 11 | 4 |
| 14 | d | 7 kl. | | 26 | 12 | 14 | Jere. 1 | Titus. 1 |
| 3 | e | 6 kl. | | 27 | Jerem. 2 | 15 | 3 | 2, 3 |
| | f | 5 kl. | | 28 | 4 | 16 | 5 | Philem. 1 |
| 11 | g | 4 kl. | | 29 | 6 | 17 | 7 | Hebreo. 1 |
| | A | 3 kl. | | 30 | 8 | 18 | 9 | 2 |
| 14 | b | *Prid.* kl. | | 30 | 10 | 19 | 11 | 3 |

## SECOND PRAYER-BOOK OF EDWARD VI. 1552.

### AUGUST HATH XXXI. DAYS.

| | | | | Psalms | MORNING PRAYER | | EVENING PRAYER | |
|---|---|---|---|---|---|---|---|---|
| | | | | | 1 Lesson. | 2 Lesson. | 1 Lesson. | 2 Lesson. |
| 8 | c | Kalend. | Lammas. | 1 | Jere. 12 | Iohn. 20 | Jer. 13 | Hebr. 4 |
| 16 | d | 4 No. | | 2 | 14 | 21 | 15 | 5 |
| 5 | e | 3 No. | | 3 | 16 | Actes 1 | 17 | 6 |
| | f | Prid. No. | | 4 | 18 | 2 | 19 | 7 |
| 13 | g | Nonas. | | 5 | 20 | 3 | 21 | 8 |
| 2 | A | 8 Id. | | 6 | 22 | 4 | 23 | 9 |
| | b | 7 Id. | | 7 | 24 | 5 | 25 | 10 |
| 10 | c | 6 Id. | | 8 | 26 | 6 | 27 | 11 |
| | d | 5 Id. | | 9 | 28 | 7 | 29 | 12 |
| 18 | e | 4 Id. | S. Lau- | 10 | 30 | 8 | 31 | 13 |
| 7 | f | 3 Id. | [rence. | 11 | 32 | 9 | 33 | Jacobi. 1 |
| | g | Prid. Id. | | 12 | 34 | 10 | 35 | 2 |
| 15 | A | Idus. | [bris. | 13 | 36 | 11 | 37 | 3 |
| 4 | b | 19 kl. | Septem- | 14 | 38 | 12 | 39 | 4 |
| | c | 18 kl. | Sol in | 15 | 40 | 13 | 41 | 5 |
| 12 | d | 17 kl. | [virgo. | 16 | 42 | 14 | 43 | 1 Peter. 1 |
| 1 | e | 16 kl. | | 17 | 44 | 15 | 45. 46 | 2 |
| | f | 15 kl. | | 18 | 47 | 16 | 48 | 3 |
| 9 | g | 14 kl. | | 19 | 49 | 17 | 50 | 4 |
| | A | 13 kl. | | 20 | 51 | 18 | 52 | 5 |
| 17 | b | 12 kl. | | 21 | Lament 1 | 19 | Lamen. 2 | 2 Pete. 1 |
| 6 | c | 11 kl. | | 22 | 3 | 20 | 4 | 2 |
| | d | 10 kl. | | 23 | 5 | 21 | Ezech. 2 | 3 |
| 13 | e | 9 kl. | Bartho. | 24 | Ezech. 3 | 22 | 6 | 1 Ihon 1 |
| 3 | f | 8 kl. | [apo. | 25 | 7 | 23 | 13 | 2 |
| | g | 7 kl. | | 26 | 14 | 24 | 18 | 3 |
| 11 | A | 6 kl. | | 27 | 33 | 25 | 34 | 4 |
| | b | 5 kl. | | 28 | Daniel 1 | 26 | Dani. 2 | 5 |
| 19 | c | 4 kl. | | 29 | 3 | 27 | 4 | 2.3 Ihon. |
| 8 | d | 3 kl. | | 30 | 5 | 28 | 6 | Jude 1 |
| | e | Prid. kl. | | 30 | 7 | Matth. 1 | 8 | Roma. 1 |

## SEPTEMBER HATH XXX. DAYS.

|    |   |           |            | Psalms | MORNING PRAYER. | | EVENING PRAYER. | |
|----|---|-----------|------------|--------|-----------------|---|-----------------|---|
|    |   |           |            |        | 1 *Lesson.*     | 2 *Lesson.* | 1 *Lesson.* | 2 *Lesson.* |
| 16 | f | *Kalend.* |            | 1      | Daniel 9        | Matth. 2    | Dani. 10    | Roma. 2 |
| 5  | g | 4 No.     |            | 2      | 11              | 3           | 12          | 3 |
|    | A | 3 No.     |            | 3      | 13              | 4           | 14          | 4 |
| 13 | b | Prid. No. |            | 4      | Ozee. 1         | 5           | Oz. 2. 3    | 5 |
| 2  | c | *Nonas.*  | Dog daies  | 5      | 4               | 6           | 5. 6        | 6 |
|    | d | 8 Id.     | [en.       | 6      | 7               | 7           | 8           | 7 |
| 10 | e | 7 Id.     |            | 7      | 9               | 8           | 10          | 8 |
|    | f | 6 Id.     |            | 8      | 11              | 9           | 12          | 9 |
| 18 | g | 5 Id.     |            | 9      | 13              | 10          | 14          | 10 |
| 7  | A | 4 Id.     |            | 10     | Joel. 1         | 11          | Joel. 2     | 11 |
|    | b | 3 Id.     |            | 11     | 3               | 12          | Amos 1      | 12 |
| 15 | c | Prid. Id. |            | 12     | Amos. 2         | 13          | 3           | 13 |
| 4  | d | *Idus.*   |            | 13     | 4               | 14          | 5           | 14 |
|    | e | 18 kl.    | Octobris.  | 14     | 6               | 15          | 7           | 15 |
| 12 | f | 17 kl.    | *Sol in Libr* | 15 | 8               | 16          | 9           | 16 |
| 1  | g | 16 kl.    |            | 16     | Abdias. 1       | 17          | Jonas. 1    | 1 Corin. 1 |
|    | A | 15 kl.    |            | 17     | Ihon 2. 3       | 18          | 4           | 2 |
| 9  | b | 14 kl.    |            | 18     | Miche. 1        | 19          | Mich. 2     | 3 |
|    | c | 13 kl.    |            | 19     | 3               | 20          | 4           | 4 |
| 17 | d | 12 kl.    |            | 20     | 5               | 21          | 6           | 5 |
| 6  | e | 11 kl.    | *S. Mat-*  | 21     | 7               | 22          | Naum. 1     | 6 |
|    | f | 10 kl.    | [*thew.*   | 22     | Naum. 2         | 23          | 3           | 7 |
| 14 | g | 9 kl.     |            | 23     | Abacuc. 1       | 24          | Abac. 2     | 8 |
| 3  | A | 8 kl.     |            | 24     | 3               | 25          | Soph. 1     | 9 |
|    | b | 7 kl.     |            | 25     | Sopho. 2        | 26          | 3           | 10 |
| 11 | c | 6 kl.     |            | 26     | Agge. 1         | 27          | Agge. 2     | 11 |
|    | d | 5 kl.     |            | 27     | Zachari. 1      | 28          | Zac. 2. 3   | 12 |
| 19 | e | 4 kl.     |            | 28     | 4. 5            | Marke 1     | 6           | 13 |
| 8  | f | 3 kl.     | *S. Michael.* | 29  | 7               | 2           | 8           | 14 |
|    | g | *Prid.* kl. |          | 30     | 9               | 3           | 10          | 15 |

## OCTOBER HATH XXXI. DAYS.

| | | | | *Psalms.* | MORNING PRAYER. | | EVENING PRAYER. | |
|---|---|---|---|---|---|---|---|---|
| | | | | | 1 *Lesson.* | 2 *Lesson.* | 1 *Lesson.* | 2 *Lesson.* |
| 16 | A | *Kalend.* | | 1 | zachar.11 | Mark 4 | Zach. 12 | 1 Cor. 16 |
| 5 | b | 6 No. | | 2 | 13 | 5 | 14 | 2 Cor. 1 |
| 13 | c | 5 No. | | 3 | Malach.1 | 6 | Mala. 2 | 2 |
| 2 | d | 4 No. | | 4 | 3 | 7 | 4 | 3 |
| | e | 3 No. | | 5 | Toby. 1 | 8 | Toby. 2 | 4 |
| 10 | f | Prid. No. | | 6 | 3 | 9 | 4 | 5 |
| | g | *Nonas.* | | 7 | 5 | 10 | 6 | 6 |
| 18 | A | 8 Id. | | 8 | 7 | 11 | 8 | 7 |
| 7 | b | 7 Id. | *Terme* | 9 | 9 | 12 | 10 | 8 |
| | c | 6 Id. | *[begin.* | 10 | 11 | 13 | 12 | 9 |
| 15 | d | 5 Id. | | 11 | 13 | 14 | 14 | 10 |
| 4 | e | 4 Id. | | 12 | Judith 1 | 15 | Judit. 2 | 11 |
| | f | 3 Id. | | 13 | 3 | 16 | 4 | 12 |
| 12 | g | Prid. Id. | *Solin Scor.* | 14 | 5 | Luke di.1 | 6 | 13 |
| 1 | A | *Idus.* | | 15 | 7 | di. 1 | 8 | Gala. 1 |
| | b | 17 kl. | Novembris | 16 | 9 | 2 | 10 | 2 |
| 9 | c | 16 kl. | | 17 | 11 | 3 | 12 | 3 |
| | d | 15 kl. | *Luke* | 18 | 13 | 4 | 14 | 4 |
| 17 | e | 14 kl. | *[Evan.* | 19 | 15 | 5 | 16 | 5 |
| 6 | f | 13 kl. | | 20 | Sapien. 1 | 6 | Sapi. 2 | 6 |
| | g | 12 kl. | | 21 | 3 | 7 | 4 | Ephesi. 1 |
| 14 | A | 11 kl. | | 22 | 5 | 8 | 6 | 2 |
| 3 | b | 10 kl. | | 23 | 7 | 9 | 8 | 3 |
| | c | 9 kl. | | 24 | 9 | 10 | 10 | 4 |
| 11 | d | 8 kl. | | 25 | 11 | 11 | 12 | 5 |
| | e | 7 kl. | | 26 | 13 | 12 | 14 | 6 |
| 19 | f | 6 kl. | | 27 | 15 | 13 | 16 | Philip. 1 |
| 8 | g | 5 kl. | *Simon &* | 28 | 17 | 14 | 18 | 2 |
| | A | 4 kl. | *[Ju.* | 29 | 19 | 15 | Eccls. 1 | 3 |
| 16 | b | 3 kl. | | 30 | Eccle. 2 | 16 | 3 | 4 |
| 5 | c | *Prid.* kl. | | 30 | 4 | 17 | 5 | Collos. 1 |

## NOVEMBER HATH XXX. DAYS.

| | | | | *Psalms.* | MORNING PRAYER. | | EVENING PRAYER. | |
|---|---|---|---|---|---|---|---|---|
| | | | | | 1 *Lesson.* | 2 *Lesson.* | 1 *Lesson.* | 2 *Lesson.* |
|    | d | *Kalend.* | *All*       | 1  | Sapie. 3 | Heb11 12 | Sapi. 5 | Apoc. 19 |
| 13 | e | 4 No.     | [*Sainctes.*| 2  | Eccles. 6 | Luk. 18 | Eccl. 7 | Collo. 2 |
| 2  | f | 3 No.     |             | 3  | 8        | 19       | 9       | 3        |
|    | g | Prid. No. |             | 4  | 10       | 20       | 11      | 4        |
| 10 | A | *Nonas.*  |             | 5  | 12       | 21       | 13      | 1 Thes. 1 |
|    | b | 8 Id.     |             | 6  | 14       | 22       | 15      | 2        |
| 18 | c | 7 Id.     |             | 7  | 16       | 23       | 17      | 3        |
| 7  | d | 6 Id.     |             | 8  | 18       | 24       | 19      | 4        |
|    | e | 5 Id.     |             | 9  | 20       | Ihon 1   | 21      | 5        |
| 15 | f | 4 Id.     |             | 10 | 22       | 2        | 23      | 2 Thes. 1 |
| 4  | g | 3 Id.     |             | 11 | 24       | 3        | 25      | 2        |
|    | A | Prid. Id. |             | 12 | 26       | 4        | 27      | 3        |
| 12 | b | *Idus.*   | *Sol in Sag.* | 13 | 28     | 5        | 29      | 1 Timo. 1 |
| 1  | c | 18 kl.    | December.   | 14 | 30       | 6        | 31      | 2. 3     |
|    | d | 17 kl.    |             | 15 | 32       | 7        | 33      | 4        |
| 9  | e | 16 kl.    |             | 16 | 34       | 8        | 35      | 5        |
|    | f | 15 kl.    |             | 17 | 36       | 9        | 37      | 6        |
| 17 | g | 14 kl.    |             | 18 | 38       | 10       | 39      | 2 Tim. 1 |
| 6  | A | 13 kl.    |             | 19 | 40       | 11       | 41      | 2        |
|    | b | 12 kl.    |             | 20 | 42       | 12       | 43      | 3        |
| 14 | c | 11 kl.    |             | 21 | 44       | 13       | 45      | 4        |
| 3  | d | 10 kl.    |             | 22 | 46       | 14       | 47      | Titus 1  |
|    | e | 9 kl.     | S. Clement. | 23 | 48       | 15       | 49      | 2. 3     |
| 11 | f | 8 kl.     |             | 24 | 50       | 16       | 51      | Phile. 1 |
|    | g | 7 kl.     |             | 25 | Baruch 1 | 17       | Baru. 2 | Hebr. 1  |
| 19 | A | 6 kl.     |             | 26 | 3        | 18       | 4       | 2        |
| 8  | b | 5 kl.     | [*ende*     | 27 | 5        | 19       | 6       | 3        |
|    | c | 4 kl.     | *Terme*     | 28 | Esay. 1  | 20       | Esay. 2 | 4        |
| 16 | d | 3 kl.     | [*Apo.*     | 29 | 3        | 21       | 4       | 5        |
| 5  | e | Prid. kl. | *Andrew*    | 30 | 5        | Actes 1  | 6       | 6        |

## DECEMBER HATH XXXI. DAYS.

| | | | Psalms. | MORNING PRAYER. | | EVENING PRAYER. | |
|---|---|---|---|---|---|---|---|
| | | | | 1 Lesson. | 2 Lesson. | 1 Lesson. | 2 Lesson. |
| | f | Kalend. | 1 | Esay. 7 | Actes 2 | Esai. 8 | Hebr. 7 |
| 13 | g | 4 No. | 2 | 9 | 3 | 10 | 8 |
| 2 | A | 3 No. | 3 | 11 | 4 | 12 | 9 |
| 10 | b | Prid. No. | 4 | 13 | 5 | 14 | 10 |
| | c | Nonas. | 5 | 15 | 6 | 16 | 11 |
| 18 | d | 8 Id. | 6 | 17 | di. 7 | 18 | 12 |
| 7 | e | 7 Id. | 7 | 19 | di. 7 | 20. 21 | 13 |
| | f | 6 Id. | 8 | 22 | 8 | 23 | James. 1 |
| 15 | g | 5 Id. | 9 | 24 | 9 | 25 | 2 |
| 4 | A | 4 Id. | 10 | 26 | 10 | 27 | 3 |
| | b | 3 Id. | 11 | 28 | 11 | 29 | 4 |
| 12 | c | Prid. Id. Sol in Cap. | 12 | 30 | 12 | 31 | 5 |
| 1 | d | Idus. | 13 | 32 | 13 | 33 | 1 Peter. 1 |
| | e | 19 kl. Januarii. | 14 | 34 | 14 | 35 | 2 |
| 9 | f | 18 kl. | 15 | 36 | 15 | 37 | 3 |
| | g | 17 kl. | 16 | 38 | 16 | 39 | 4 |
| 17 | A | 16 kl. | 17 | 40 | 17 | 41 | 5 |
| 6 | b | 15 kl. | 18 | 42 | 18 | 43 | 2 Peter. 1 |
| | c | 14 kl. | 19 | 44 | 19 | 45 | 2 |
| 14 | d | 13 kl. | 20 | 46 | 20 | 47 | 3 |
| 3 | e | 12 kl. Thomas | 21 | 48 | 21 | 49 | 1 Ihon. 1 |
| | f | 11 kl. [Ap. | 22 | 50 | 22 | 51 | 2 |
| 11 | g | 10 kl. | 23 | 52 | 23 | 53 | 3 |
| | A | 9 kl. | 24 | 54 | 24 | 55 | 4 |
| 19 | b | 8 kl. Christmas | 25 | Esay. 9 | Luke 22 | Esay. 7 | Titus. 3 |
| 8 | c | 7 kl. S. Stephan | 26 | 56 | Ac. 6. 7 | 57 | Actes 7 |
| | d | 6 kl. S. Jhon Ev. | 27 | 58 | Apocali 1 | 59 | Apo. 22 |
| 16 | e | 5 kl. Innocentes | 28 | Jere. 31 | Acte 25 | Esay. 60 | 1 Ihon. 5 |
| 5 | f | 4 kl. | 29 | Esaie 61 | 26 | 62 | 2 Ihon. 1 |
| | g | 3 kl. | 30 | 63 | 27 | 64 | 3 Ihon. 1 |
| 13 | A | Prid. kl. | 30 | 65 | 28 | 66 | Jude. 1 |

## THE ORDER WHERE

### MORNING AND EVENING PRAYER SHALL BE USED AND SAID.

*The morning, and evening prayer, shall be used in such place of the Church, Chapel, or Chancel, and the Minister shall so turn him, as the people may best hear. And if there be any controversy therein, the matter shall be referred to the ordinary, and he or his deputy shall appoint the place, and the chancels shall remain, as they have done in times past.*

*And here is to be noted, that the minister at the time of the communion, and at all other times in his ministration, shall use neither Alb, Vestment, nor Cope: but being Archbishop, or Bishop, he shall have and wear a rochet: and being a priest or Deacon, he shall have and wear a surplice only.*

### The Sunday called Septuagesima.
#### The Collect.

O LORD, we beseech thee favourably to hear the prayers of thy people, that we which are justly punished for our offences, may be mercifully delivered by thy goodness, for the glory of thy name, through Jesu Christ our Saviour, who liveth and reigneth world without end.

*The Epistle.* 1 Cor. ix. Perceive ye not, how that they . . . . . [&c.]
[i.e. 1 Cor. ix. verse 24 to the end.]

*The Gospel.* Math. xx. The kingdom of heaven is like unto a man . . . . . [&c.]
[i.e. Matt. xx. verse 1 to verse 17.]

### The Sunday called Sexagesima.
#### The Collect.

LORD God, which seest that we put not our trust in any thing that we do: mercifully grant that by thy power we may be defended against all adversity, through Jesus Christ our Lord.

*The Epistle.* 2 Cor. xi. Ye suffer fools gladly . . . [&c.]
[i.e. 2 Cor. xi. verse 19 to verse 32.]

*The Gospel.* Luc. viii. When much people were gathered . . . . . [&c.]
[i.e. Luke viii. verse 4 to verse 16.]

### The Sunday called Quinquagesima.
#### The Collect.

O LORD, which dost teach us, that all our doings without charity are nothing worth: send thy Holy Ghost, and pour in our hearts that most excellent gift of charity, the very bond of peace and all virtues, without the which, whosoever liveth is counted dead before thee: Grant this, for thy only Son Jesus Christ's sake.

*The Epistle.* 1 Cor. xiii. Though I speak with tongues of men ..... [&c.]
[i.e. 1 Cor. xiii. verse 1 to the end.]

*The Gospel.* Luk. xviii. Jesus took unto him the twelve ..... [&c.]
[i.e. Luke xviii. verse 31 to the end.]

### *The first day of Lent.*
#### *The Collect.*

ALMIGHTY and everlasting God, which hatest nothing that thou hast made, and dost forgive the sins of all them that be penitent: Create and make in us new and contrite hearts, that we worthily lamenting our sins, and knowledging our wretchedness, may obtain of thee, the God of all mercy, perfect remission and forgiveness, through Jesus Christ.

*The Epistle.* Joel ii. Turn you unto me with all your hearts ..... [&c.]
[i.e. Joel ii. verse 12 to verse 17.]

*The Gospel.* Math. vi. When ye fast be not sad as the hypocrites are ..... [&c.]
[i.e. Matt. vi. verse 16 to verse 22.]

### *The first Sunday in Lent.*
#### *The Collect.*

O LORD, which for our sake didst fast forty days and forty nights: Give us grace to use such abstinence, that our flesh being subdued to the Spirit, we may ever obey thy godly motions\*, in righteousness and true holiness, to thy honour and glory, which livest and reignest. &c.

*The Epistle.* 2 Cor. vi. We as helpers exhort you that ye receive not ..... [&c.]
[i.e. 2 Cor. vi. verse 1 to verse 11.]

\* In some copies, "monitions."

*The Gospel.* Math. iv. Then was Jesus led away of the Spirit ..... [&c.]
[i.e. Matth. iv. verse 1 to verse 12.]

### *The second Sunday* [f].

#### *The Collect.*

ALMIGHTY God, which dost see that we have no power of ourselves to help ourselves: keep thou us both outwardly in our bodies, and inwardly in our souls, that we may be defended from all adversities which may happen to the body, and from all evil thoughts which may assault and hurt the soul; through Jesus Christ. &c.

*The Epistle.* 1 Thess. iv. We beseech you brethren and exhort ..... [&c.]
[i.e. 1 Thess. iv. verse 1 to verse 9.]

*The Gospel.* Math. xv. Jesus went thence .... [&c.]
[i.e. Matth. xv. verse 21 to verse 29.]

### *The third Sunday* [f].

#### *The Collect.*

WE beseech thee, almighty God, look upon the hearty desires of thy humble servants: and stretch forth the right hand of thy majesty, to be our defence against all our enemies: through Jesus Christ our Lord.

*The Epistle.* Ephe. v. Be ye the followers of God ..... [&c.]
[i.e. Ephes. v. verse 1 to verse 15.]

*The Gospel.* Luke xi. Jesus was casting out a devil that was dumb ..... [&c.]
[i.e. Luke xi. verse 14 to verse 26.]

[f] In some copies, "Sunday in Lent."

### *The fourth Sunday* [s].
#### *The Collect.*

GRANT, we beseech thee, almighty God, that we, which for our evil deeds are worthily punished, by the comfort of thy grace may mercifully be relieved: through our Lord Jesus Christ.

*The Epistle.* Gala. iv. Tell me, ye that desire, [&c.]
[i.e. Gal. iv. verse 21 to the end.]

*The Gospel.* John vi. Jesus departed over the sea of Galilee . . . . . [&c.]
[i.e. John vi. verse 1 to verse 15.]

### *The fifth Sunday* [s].
#### *The Collect.*

WE beseech thee, almighty God, mercifully to look upon thy people: that by thy great goodness they may be governed and preserved evermore, both in body and soul, through Jesus Christ our Lord.

*The Epistle.* Hebre. ix. Christ being an high-priest . . . . . [&c.]
[i.e. Heb. ix. verse 11 to verse 16.]

*The Gospel.* John viii. Which of you can rebuke me of sin . . . . . [&c.]
[i.e. John viii. verse 46 to the end.]

### *The Sunday next before Easter.*
#### *The Collect.*

ALMIGHTY and everlasting God, which of thy tender love towards man, has sent our Saviour Jesus Christ to take upon him our flesh, and to suffer death upon the cross, that all mankind should follow the example

---
[s] In some copies, "in Lent" is added.

of his great humility: mercifully grant, that we both follow the example of his patience, and be made partakers of his resurrection: through the same Jesus Christ our Lord.

*The Epistle.* Philip. ii. Let the same mind be in you..... [&c.]
[i.e. Phil. ii. verse 5 to verse 12.]

*The Gospel.* Math. xxvi. and xxvii. And it came to pass..... [&c.]
[i.e. Matt. xxvi. verse 1 to chap. xxvii. verse 57.]

### *Monday before Easter.*

*The Epistle.* Esai. lxiii. What is he this that cometh..... [&c.]
[i.e. Esai. lxiii. verse 1 to the end.]

*The Gospel.* Mar. xiv. After two days was Easter and the dayes..... [&c.]
[i.e. Mark xiv. verse 1 to the end.]

### *Tuesday before Easter.*

*The Epistle.* Esai. l. The Lord God hath opened mine ear..... [&c.]
[i.e. Esai. l. verse 5 to the end.]

*The Gospel.* Mar. xv. And anon in the dawning the high priests..... [&c.]
[i.e. Mark xv. verse 1 to the end.]

### *Wednesday before Easter.*

*The Epistle.* Hebr. ix. Whereas is a testament there must also..... [&c.]
[i.e. Hebr. ix. verse 16 to the end.]

*The Gospel.* Luk. xxii. The feast of sweet bread which is called Easter..... [&c.]
[i.e. Luke xxii. verse 1 to the end.]

### *Thursday before Easter.*

*The Epistle.* 1 Cor. xi. This I warn you of and commend not that .... [&c.]

[i.e. 1 Cor. xi. verse 17 to the end.]

*The Gospel.* Luk. xxiii. The whole multitude of them ..... [&c.]

[i.e. Luke xxiii. ver. 1 to the end.]

### *On Good Friday.*

#### *The Collects.*

ALMIGHTY God, we beseech thee graciously to behold this thy family, for the which our Lord Jesus Christ was contented to be betrayed, and given up into the hands of wicked men, and to suffer death upon the cross: who liveth and reigneth, &c.

ALMIGHTY and everlasting God, by whose Spirit the whole body of the Church is governed and sanctified: receive our supplications and prayers, which we offer before thee for all estates of men in thy holy congregation, that every member of the same, in his vocation and ministry, may truly and godly serve thee: through our Lord Jesus Christ.

MERCIFUL God, who hast made all men, and hatest nothing that thou hast made, nor wouldest the death of a sinner, but rather that he should be converted and live: have mercy upon all Jews, Turks, Infidels, and Heretics, and take from them all ignorance, hardness of heart, and contempt of thy word: and so fetch them home, blessed Lord, to thy flock, that they may be saved among the remnant of the true Israelites, and be made one fold under one shepherd, Jesus Christ our Lord: who liveth and reigneth, &c.

*The Epistle.* Hebre. x. The law which hath but a shadow ..... [&c.]
[i.e. Heb. x. verse 1 to verse 26.]

*The Gospel.* John xviii. When Jesus had spoken these words ..... [&c.]
[i.e. John xviii. verse 1 to end of chap. xix.]

### Easter Even.

*The Epistle.* 1 Pet. iii. It is better ..... [&c.]
[i.e. 1 Pet. iii. verse 17 to the end.]

*The Gospel.* Mathew xxvii. When the even .. [&c.]
[i.e. Matt. xxvii. verse 57 to the end.]

### Easter day.

*At Morning Prayer instead of the Psalm,* O come, let us, &c. *These Anthems shall be sung or said.*

CHRIST rising again from the dead, now dieth not. Death from henceforth hath no power upon him. For in that he died, he died but once to put away sin: but in that he liveth, he liveth unto God. And so likewise, count[h] yourselves dead unto sin, but living unto God in Christ Jesus our Lord.

CHRIST is risen again, the firstfruits of them that sleep : for seeing that by man came death, by man also cometh the resurrection of the dead. For as by Adam all men do die, so by Christ all men shall be restored to life.

### The Collect.

ALMIGHTY God, which through thy only begotten Son Jesus Christ hast overcome death, and opened unto us the gate of everlasting life: we humbly beseech thee, that as by thy special grace, preventing us, thou dost put in our minds good desires; so by

---
[h] In some copies, "account."

thy continual help we may bring the same to good effect, through Jesus Christ our Lord: who liveth and reigneth, &c.

*The Epistle.* Coloss. iii. If ye be risen again with Christ . . . . . [&c.]
[i.e. Col. iii. verse 1 to verse 8.]

*The Gospel.* John xx. The first day of the Sabbaths . . . . . [&c.]
[i.e. John xx. verse 1 to verse 11.]

### *Monday in Easter Week.*

#### *The Collect.*

ALMIGHTY God, which through thy only begotten Son Jesus Christ, hast overcome death, and opened unto us the gate of everlasting life: we humbly beseech thee, that as by thy special grace, preventing us, thou dost put in our minds good desires; so by thy continual help we may bring the same to good effect, through Jesus Christ our Lord: who liveth and reigneth, &c.

*The Epistle.* Acts x. Peter opened his mouth and said . . . . . [&c.]
[i.e. Acts x. verse 34 to verse 44.]

*The Gospel.* Luk. xxiv. Behold two of the disciples went . . . . . [&c.]
[i.e. Luke xxiv. verse 13 to verse 36.]

### *Tuesday in Easter Week.*

#### *The Collect.*

ALMIGHTY Father, which hast given thy only Son to die for our sins, and to rise again for our justification: Grant us so to put away the leaven of malice and wickedness, that we may alway serve thee in pureness of living and truth: through Jesus Christ our Lord.

*The Epistle.* Acts. xiii. Ye men and brethren .. [&c.]
[i.e. Acts xiii. verse 26 to verse 42.]

*The Gospel.* Lu. xxiv. Jesus stood in the midst of his disciples . . . . . [&c.]
[i.e. Luke xxiv. verse 36 to verse 49.]

### *The first Sunday after Easter.*
#### *The Collect.*

ALMIGHTY God, &c. *As at the Communion on Easter Day.*

*The Epistle.* 1 John v. All that is born of God . . . [&c.]
[i.e. 1 John v. verse 4 to verse 13.]

*The Gospel.* John xx. The same day at night . . . [&c.]
[i.e. John xx. verse 19 to verse 24.]

### *The second Sunday after Easter.*
#### *The Collect.*

ALMIGHTY God, which hast given thy holy Son to be unto us, both a sacrifice for sin, and also an example of godly life: Give us the grace that we may always most thankfully receive that his inestimable benefit, and also daily endeavour ourselves to follow the blessed steps of his most holy life.

*The Epistle.* 1 Peter ii. This is thankworthy . . . [&c.]
[i.e. 1 Pet. ii. verse 19 to the end.]

*The Gospel.* John x. Christ said to his disciples I am the good shepherd . . . . . [&c.]
[i.e. John x. verse 11 to verse 17.]

### *The third Sunday.*
#### *The Collect.*

ALMIGHTY God, which shewest to all men that be in error the light of thy truth, to the intent that they may return into the way of righteousness: Grant unto all them that be admitted into the fellowship of Christ's religion, that they may eschew those things that be contrary to their profession, and follow all such things as be agreeable to the same: through our Lord Jesus Christ.

*The Epistle.* 1 Peter ii. Dearly beloved, I beseech you . . . . . [&c.]
[i.e. 1 Pet. ii. verse 11 to verse 18.]

*The Gospel.* John xvi. Jesus said to his disciples After a while . . . . . [&c.]
[i.e. John xvi. verse 6 to verse 23.]

### *The fourth Sunday.*

#### *The Collect.*

ALMIGHTY God, which dost make the minds of all faithful men to be of one will: grant unto thy people, that they may love the thing, which thou commandest, and desire that which thou dost promise: that among the sundry and manifold changes of the world, our hearts may surely there be fixed, where as true joys are to be found: Through Christ our Lord.

*The Epistle.* James i. Every good gift . . . . . [&c.]
[i.e. James i. verse 17 to verse 22.]

*The Gospel.* John xvi. Jesus said unto his disciples . . . . . [&c.]
[i.e. John xvi. verse 5 to verse 15.]

### *The fifth Sunday.*

#### *The Collect.*

LORD, from whom all good things do come; grant us thy humble servants, that by thy holy inspiration we may think those things that be good, and by thy merciful guiding may perform the same[1]; through our Lord Jesus Christ.

*The Epistle.* James i. See that ye be doers of the word . . . . . [&c.]
[i.e. James i. verse 22 to the end.]

[1] In some copies, "the same" omitted.

*The Gospel.* John xvi. Verily, verily I say unto you . . . . . [&c.]
[i.e. John xvi. verse 23 to the end.]

### *The Ascension Day.*
#### *The Collect.*

GRANT, we beseech thee, almighty God, that like as we do believe thy only begotten Son our Lord to have ascended into the heavens: so we may also in heart and mind thither ascend, and with him continually dwell.

*The Epistle.* Acts i. In the former treatise . . . [&c.]
[i.e. Acts i. verse 1 to verse 12.]
*The Gospel.* Mar. xvi. Jesus appeared unto the eleven . . . . . [&c.]
[i.e. Mark xvi. verse 14 to the end.]

### *The Sunday after the Ascension day.*
#### *The Collect.*

O GOD, the King of glory, which hast exalted thine only Son, Jesus Christ, with great triumph unto thy kingdom in heaven: we beseech thee leave us not comfortless, but send to us thine Holy Ghost to comfort us, and exalt us unto the same place, whither our Saviour Christ is gone before; who liveth and reigneth, &c.

*The Epistle.* 1 Peter iv. The end of all things is at hand . . . . . [&c.]
[i.e. 1 Pet. iv. verse 7 to verse 12.]
*The Gospel.* John xv., John xvi. When the Comforter is come . . . . . [&c.]
[i.e. John xv. verse 26, and chap. xvi. to middle of verse 4.]

### *Whitsunday.*
#### *The Collect.*

GOD, which as upon this day hast taught the hearts of thy faithful people, by the sending to them the light of thy Holy Spirit: Grant us by the same Spirit to have a right judgment in all things, and evermore to rejoice in his holy comfort, through the merits of Christ Jesu our Saviour, who liveth and reigneth with thee in the unity of the same Spirit one God, world without end.

*The Epistle.* Acts ii. When the fifty days were come..... [&c.]
[i.e. Acts ii. verse 1 to verse 12.]

*The Gospel.* John xiv. Jesus said unto his disciples..... [&c.]
[i.e. John xiv. verse 15 to verse 22.]

### *Monday in Whitsun-week.*

*The Collect.*

GOD, which [k], &c., (*As upon Whitsunday.*)

*The Epistle.* Acts x. Then Peter opened his mouth and said..... [&c.]
[i.e. Acts x. verse 34 to the end.]

*The Gospel.* John iii. So God loved the world, [&c.]
[i.e. John iii. verse 16 to verse 22.]

### *The Tuesday after Whitsunday.*

*The Collect.*

GOD, which, &c., (*As upon Whitsunday.*)

*The Epistle.* Acts viii. When the Apostles which were at Jerusalem..... [&c.]
[i.e. Acts viii. verse 14 to verse 18.]

*The Gospel.* John x. Verily, verily I say unto you..... [&c.]
[i.e. John x. verse 1 to verse 11.]

### *Trinity Sunday.*

*The Collect.*

ALMIGHTY and everlasting God, which hast given unto us thy servants grace by the confession of a

---

[k] In some copies, "God which has given, &c., as upon Whitsunday."

true faith to acknowledge the glory of the eternal Trinity, and in the power of the divine Majesty to worship the Unity: we beseech thee that through the steadfastness of this faith, we may evermore be defended from all adversity: which livest and reignest, one God, world without end. Amen.

*The Epistle.* Apoc. iv. After this I looked, and behold ..... [&c.]

[i.e. Apoc. iv. verse 1 to the end.]

*The Gospel.* John iii. There was a man of the Pharisees ..... [&c.]

[i.e. John iii. verse 1 to verse 16.]

### *The first Sunday after Trinity Sunday.*

#### *The Collect.*

GOD, the strength of all them that trust in thee, mercifully accept our prayers; and because the weakness of our mortal nature can do no good thing without thee, grant us the help of thy grace, that in keeping of thy commandments, we may please thee both in will and deed; through Jesus Christ our Lord.

*The Epistle.* 1 John iv. Dearly beloved, let us love one another ..... [&c.]

[i.e. 1 John iv. verse 7 to the end.]

*The Gospel.* Luk. xvi. There was a certain rich man ..... [&c.]

[i.e. Luke xvi. verse 19 to the end.]

### *The Second Sunday.*

#### *The Collect.*

LORD, make us to have a perpetual fear and love of thy holy name: for thou never failest to help and govern them whom thou dost bring up in thy steadfast love. Grant this, &c.

*The Epistle.* 1 John iii. Marvel not, my brethren though the world..... [&c.]
[i.e. 1 John iii. verse 13 to the end.]

*The Gospel.* Luke xiv. A certain man ordained a great supper..... [&c.]
[i.e. Luke xiv. verse 16 to verse 25.]

### *The third Sunday.*

#### *The Collect.*

LORD, we beseech thee mercifully to hear us, and unto whom thou hast given an hearty desire to pray, grant that by thy mighty aid we may be defended: through Jesus Christ our Lord.

*The Epistle.* 1 Peter v. Submit yourselves every man..... [&c.]
[1 Peter v. verse 5 to verse 12.]

*The Gospel.* Luke xv. Then resorted unto him..[&c.]
[i.e. Luke xv. verse 1 to verse 11.]

### *The fourth Sunday.*

#### *The Collect.*

GOD, the Protector of all that trust in thee, without whom nothing is strong, nothing is holy: increase and multiply upon us thy mercy, that thou being our ruler and guide, we may so pass through things temporal, that we finally lose not the things eternal: grant this, heavenly Father, for Jesu Christ's sake our Lord.

*The Epistle.* Rom. viii. I suppose that the afflictions..... [&c.]
[i.e. Rom. viii. verse 18 to verse 24.]

*The Gospel.* Luke vi. Be ye merciful, as your Father..... [&c.]
[i.e. Luke vi. verse 36 to verse 43.]

### The fifth Sunday.
#### The Collect.

GRANT Lord, we beseech thee, that the course of this world may be so peaceably ordered by thy governance, that thy congregation may joyfully serve thee in all godly quietness: through Jesus Christ our Lord.

*The Epistle.* 1 Peter iii. Be you all of one mind and of one heart . . . . . [&c.]
[i.e. 1 Peter iii. verse 8 to verse 16.]

*The Gospel.* Luke v. It came to pass that . . [&c.]
[i.e. Luke v. verse 1 to verse 12.]

### The sixth Sunday.
#### The Collect.

GOD, which hast prepared to them that love thee, such good things as pass all man's understanding: Pour into our hearts such love toward thee, that we loving thee in all things, may obtain thy promises, which exceed all that we can desire; through Jesus Christ our Lord.

*The Epistle.* Rom. vi. Know ye not, that all we which are baptized . . . . . [&c.]
[i.e. Rom. vi. verse 3 to verse 12.]

*The Gospel.* Math. v. Jesus said unto his disciples, Except your righteousness . . . . . [&c.]
[i.e. Mat. v. verse 20 to verse 27.]

### The seventh Sunday.
#### The Collect.

LORD of all power and might, which art the author and giver of all good things: graff in our hearts the love of thy name, increase in us true religion, nourish us with all goodness, and of thy great mercy keep us in the same: Through Jesus Christ our Lord.

*The Epistle.* Roma. vi. I speak grossly, because of the infirmity ..... [&c.]
[i.e. Rom. vi. verse 19 to the end.]

*The Gospel.* Mar. viii. In those days, when there was ..... [&c.]
[i.e. Mark viii. verse 1 to verse 10.]

### *The eighth Sunday.*

#### *The Collect.*

God, whose providence is never deceived: we humbly beseech thee, that thou wilt put away from us all hurtful things, and give those things which be profitable for us: Through Jesus Christ our Lord.

*The Epistle.* Roma. viii. Brethren, we are debtors not to the flesh ..... [&c.]
[i.e. Rom. viii. verse 12 to verse 18.]

*The Gospel.* Mat. vii. Beware of false prophets which come ..... [&c.]
[i.e. Matt. vii. verse 15 to verse 22.]

### *The ninth Sunday.*

#### *The Collect.*

GRANT to us, Lord, we beseech thee, the spirit to think and do always such things as be rightful: that we, which cannot be without thee, may by thee be able to live according to thy will: Through Jesu Christ our Lord.

*The Epistle.* 1 Cor. x. Brethren, I would not that ..... [&c.]
[i.e. 1 Cor. x. verse 1 to verse 14.]

*The Gospel.* Luke. xvi. Jesus said to his disciples ..... [&c.]
[i.e. Luke xvi. verse 1 to verse 10.]

### *The tenth Sunday.*

#### *The Collect.*

LET thy merciful ears, O Lord, be open to the prayers of thy humble servants: and that they may obtain their petitions, make them to ask such things as shall please thee: Through Jesus Christ our Lord.

*The Epistle.* 1 Cor. xii. Concerning spiritual things . . . . . [&c.]
[i.e. 1 Cor. xii. verse 1 to verse 12.]

*The Gospel.* Luk. xix. And when he was come near . . . . . [&c.]
[i.e. Luke xix. verse 41 to verse 47.]

### *The eleventh Sunday.*

#### *The Collect.*

GOD, which declarest[1] thy almighty power, most chiefly in shewing mercy and pity: Give unto us abundantly thy grace, that we running to thy promises, may be made partakers of thy heavenly treasure: through Jesus Christ our Lord.

*The Epistle.* 1 Cor. xv. Brethren, as pertaining to the Gospel . . . . . [&c.]
[i.e. 1 Cor. xv. verse 1 to verse 12.]

*The Gospel.* Lu. xviii. Christ told this parable, [&c.]
[i.e. Luke xviii. verse 9 to verse 15.]

### *The twelfth Sunday.*

#### *The Collect.*

ALMIGHTY and everlasting God, which art always more ready to hear than we to pray: and art wont to give more than either we desire or deserve: Pour down upon us the abundance of thy mercy, forgiving us those things whereof our conscience is afraid, and giving unto us that, that our prayer dare not presume to ask: through Jesus Christ our Lord.

*The Epistle.* 2 Cor. iii. Such trust have we through Christ . . . . . [&c.]
[i.e. 2 Cor. iii. verse 4 to verse 10.]

---

[1] In some copies, "declared."

*The Gospel.* Mar. vii. Jesus departed from the coasts ..... [&c.]
[i.e. Mar. vii. verse 31 to the end.]

### *The thirteenth Sunday.*

*The Collect.*

ALMIGHTY and merciful God, of whose only gift it cometh, that thy faithful people do unto thee true and laudable service : grant, we beseech thee, that we may so run to thy heavenly promises, that we fail not finally to attain the same : Through Jesus Christ our Lord.

*The Epistle.* Galat. iii. To Abraham and his seed, [&c.]
[i.e. Gal. iii. verse 16 to verse 23.]
*The Gospel.* Luke x. Happy are the eyes which see ..... [&c.]
[i.e. Luke x. verse 23 to verse 38.]

### *The fourteenth Sunday.*

*The Collect.*

ALMIGHTY and everlasting God, give unto us the increase of faith, hope, and charity, and, that we may obtain that which thou dost promise, make us to love that which thou dost command, through Jesus [m] Christ our Lord.

*The Epistle.* Galat. v. I say walk in the Spirit, [&c.]
[i.e. Gal. v. verse 16 to verse 25.]
*The Gospel.* Lu. xvii. And it chanced as Jesus went to Jerusalem ..... [&c.]
[i.e. Luke xvii. verse 11 to verse 20.]

### *The fifteenth Sunday.*

*The Collect.*

KEEP, we beseech thee, O Lord, thy church with thy perpetual mercy, and because the frailty of man,

[m] In some copies, "Jesu."

without thee, cannot but fall: keep us ever by thy help, and lead us to all things profitable to our salvation: through Jesus Christ our Lord. Amen.

*The Epistle.* Galat. vi. Ye see how large a letter, [&c.]
[i.e. Gal. vi. verse 11 to the end.]

*The Gospel.* Math. vi. No man can serve two masters . . . . . [&c.]
[i.e. Matt. vi. verse 24 to the end.]

### *The sixteenth Sunday.*

#### *The Collect.*

LORD, we beseech thee, let thy continual pity cleanse and defend thy congregation: and because it cannot continue in safety without thy succour, preserve it evermore by thy help and goodness: through Jesus Christ our Lord.

*The Epistle.* Ephe. iii. I desire that you faint not . . . . . [&c.]
[i.e. Ephes. iii. verse 13 to the end.]

*The Gospel.* Luke vii. And it fortuned that Jesus, [&c.]
[i.e. Luke vii. verse 11 to verse 18.]

### *The seventeenth Sunday.*

#### *The Collect.*

LORD, we pray thee that thy grace may always prevent and follow us, and make us continually to be given to all good works: through Jesu[a] Christ our Lord.

*The Epistle.* Ephe. iv. I (which am a prisoner of the Lord's) . . . . . [&c.]
[i.e. Ephes. iv. verse 1 to verse 7.]

---

[a] In some copies, "Jesus."

# THE COLLECTS, &c. 53

*The Gospel.* Lu. xiv. It chanced that Jesus went..... [&c.]
[i.e. Luke xiv. verse 1 to verse 12.]

### The eighteenth Sunday.

#### The Collect.

LORD, we beseech thee, grant thy people grace to avoid the infections of the devil, and with pure heart and mind to follow thee, the only God: through Jesus Christ our Lord.

*The Epistle.* 1 Corin. i. I thank my God always.... [&c.]
[i.e. 1 Cor. i. verse 4 to verse 9.]

*The Gospel.* Mat. xxii. When the Pharisees had heard..... [&c.]
[i.e. Matt. xxii. verse 34 to the end.]

### The nineteenth Sunday.

#### The Collect.

O GOD, forasmuch as without thee we are not able to please thee: Grant that the working of thy mercy may in all things direct and rule our hearts: Through Jesus Christ our Lord.

*The Epistle.* Ephe. iv. This I say and testify through the Lord..... [&c.]
[i.e. Ephes. iv. verse 17 to the end.]

*The Gospel.* Math. ix. Jesus entered into a ship, [&c.]
[i.e. Matt. ix. verse 1 to verse 9.]

### The twentieth Sunday.

#### The Collect.

ALMIGHTY and merciful God, of thy bountiful goodness keep us from all things that may hurt us: that we being ready both in body and soul, may with free hearts accomplish those things, that thou wouldest have done: Through Jesus Christ our Lord.

*The Epistle.* Ephesi. v. Take heed therefore how ye walk . . . . . [&c.]
[i.e. Ephes. v. verse 15 to verse 22.]

*The Gospel.* Mat. xxii. Jesus said to his disciples, the kingdom of heaven . . . . . [&c.]
[i.e. Matt. xxii. verse 1 to verse 15.]

### *The twenty-first Sunday.*

#### *The Collect.*

GRANT, we beseech thee, merciful Lord, to thy faithful people pardon and peace, that they may be cleansed from all their sins, and serve thee with a quiet mind: Through Jesus Christ our Lord.

*The Epistle.* Ephes. vi. My brethren, be strong, [&c.]
[i.e. Eph. vi. verse 10 to verse 21.]

*The Gospel.* John iv. There was a certain ruler, [&c.]
[i.e. John iv. verse 46 to the end.]

### *The twenty-second Sunday.*

#### *The Collect.*

LORD, we beseech thee to keep thy household the Church in continual godliness: that through thy protection, it may be free from all adversities, and devoutly given to serve thee in good works, to the glory of thy name: Through Jesus Christ our Lord.

*The Epistle.* Philip. i. I thank my God with all remembrance of you . . . . . [&c.]
[i.e. Phil. i. verse 3 to verse 12.]

*The Gospel.* Mathew xviii. Peter said unto Jesus . . . . [&c.]
[i.e. Matt. xviii. verse 21 to the end.]

### The twenty-third Sunday.

#### The Collect.

GOD our refuge and strength, which art the author of all godliness, be ready to hear the devout prayers of thy º Church : and grant that those things which we ask faithfully, we may obtain effectually : through Jesu Christ our Lord.

*The Epistle.* Philip. iii. Brethren, be followers together ..... [&c.]

[i.e. Phil. iii. verse 17 to the end.]

*The Gospel.* Mat. xxii. Then the Pharisees went out and took counsel ..... [&c.]

[i.e. Matt. xxii. verse 15 to verse 23.]

### The twenty-fourth Sunday.

#### The Collect.

LORD, we beseech thee, assoil thy people from their offences : that through thy bountiful goodness, we may be delivered from the bands of all those sins, which by our frailty we have committed : Grant this. &c. ᴾ

*The Epistle.* Colossi. i. We give thanks to God, [&c.]

[i.e. Colos. i. verse 3 to verse 13.]

*The Gospel.* Math. ix. While Jesus spake unto the people ..... [&c.]

[i.e. Matt. ix. verse 18 to verse 27.]

### The twenty-fifth Sunday.

#### The Collect.

STIR up, we beseech thee, O Lord, the wills of thy faithful people : that they plenteously bringing forth the fruit of good works, may of thee be plenteously rewarded : through Jesus Christ our Lord ᴾ.

º In some copies, "of the church."   ᴾ In some copies, "Amen" is added.

*The Epistle.* Jer. xxiii. Behold, the time cometh ..... [&c.]

[i.e. Jer. xxiii. verse 5 to verse 9.]

*The Gospel.* John vi. When Jesus lift up his eyes ..... [&c.]

[i.e. John vi. verse 5 to verse 15.]

*If there be any more Sundays before Advent Sunday, to supply the same shall be taken the service of some of those Sundays that were omitted between the Epiphany and Septuagesima.*

### *Saint Andrew's Day.*

#### *The Collect.*

ALMIGHTY God, which didst give such grace unto thy holy apostle Saint Andrew, that he readily obeyed the calling of thy Son Jesus Christ, and followed him without delay: Grant unto us all, that we being called by thy holy word, may forthwith give over ourselves, obediently to follow thy holy commandments: through the same Jesus Christ our Lord.

*The Epistle.* Roma. x. If thou knowledge with thy mouth ..... [&c.]

[i.e. Rom. x. verse 9 to the end.]

*The Gospel.* Mat. iv. As Jesus walked by the sea of Galilee ..... [&c.]

[i.e. Matt. iv. verse 18 to verse 23.]

### *Saint Thomas the Apostle.*

#### *The Collect.*

ALMIGHTY everliving God, which for the more confirmation of the faith, didst suffer thy holy Apostle Thomas to be doubtful in thy Son's resurrection: grant us so perfectly, and without all doubt to believe in thy Son Jesus Christ, that our faith in thy sight never be reproved: hear us, O Lord, through the same Jesus Christ: to whom with thee and the Holy Ghost be all honour, &c.

*The Epistle.* Ephe. ii. Now ye are not strangers, [&c.]
[i.e. Ephes. ii. verse 19 to the end.]

*The Gospel.* John xx. Thomas one of the twelve which . . . . . [&c.]
[i.e. John xx. verse 24 to the end.]

### *The Conversion of Saint Paul.*

#### *The Collect.*

GOD, which hast taught all the world, through the preaching of thy blessed Apostle Saint Paul: grant, we beseech thee, that we which have his wonderful conversion in remembrance, may follow and fulfil thy holy doctrine that he taught: through Jesu Christ our Lord ¶.

*The Epistle.* Act. ix. And Saul yet breathing out . . . . . [&c.]
[i.e. Acts ix. verse 1 to verse 23.]

*The Gospel.* Mat. xix. Peter answered and said . . . . . [&c.]
[i.e. Matt. xix. verse 27 to the end.]

### *The Purification of Saint Mary the virgin.*

#### *The Collect.*

ALMIGHTY and everlasting God, we humbly beseech thy Majesty, that as thy only begotten Son was this day presented in the Temple, in the sub-

¶ In some copies, "Amen" is added.

stance[r] of our flesh ; so grant that we may be presented unto thee with pure and clear minds : By Jesus Christ our Lord.

### *The Epistle.*
*The same that is appointed for the Sunday.*

*The Gospel.* Luke ii. When the time of their purification ..... [&c.]

[i.e. Luke ii. verse 22 to verse 28.]

### *Saint Mathie's day.*

#### *The Collect.*

ALMIGHTY God, which in the place of the traitor Judas didst choose thy faithful servant Mathie to be of the number of thy twelve Apostles : Grant that thy church, being alway preserved from false Apostles, may be ordered and guided by faithful and true pastors : Through Jesus Christ our Lord.

*The Epistle.* Act. i. In those days Peter stood up ..... [&c.]

[i.e. Acts i. verse 15 to the end.]

*The Gospel.* Math. xi. In that time Jesus answered ..... [&c.]

[i.e. Matt. xi. verse 25 to the end.]

### *The Annunciation of the virgin Mary.*

#### *The Collect.*

WE beseech thee, Lord, pour thy grace into our hearts, that as we have known Christ thy Son's incarnation, by the message of an Angel ; so by his cross and passion, we may be brought unto the glory of his resurrection : Through the same Christ our Lord.

---

[r] In some copies, "in substance."

*The Epistle.* Esai. vii. God spake once again unto Ahaz . . . . . [&c.]
[i.e. Isai. vii. verse 10 to verse 16.]

*The Gospel.* Luc. i. And in the sixth month the angel Gabriel . . . . . [&c.]
[i.e. Luke i. verse 26 to verse 39.]

### *Saint Mark's Day.*

#### *The Collect.*

ALMIGHTY God, which hast instructed thy holy Church, with the heavenly doctrine of thy Evangelist Saint Mark: give us grace so to be established by thy holy gospel, that we be not, like children, carried away with every blast of vain doctrine: Through Jesus Christ our Lord.

*The Epistle.* Ephe. iv. Unto every one of us is given grace . . . . . [&c.]
[i.e. Eph. iv. verse 7 to verse 17.]

*The Gospel.* John xv. I am the true vine . . . [&c.]
[i.e. John xv. verse 1 to verse 12.]

### *Saint Philip and James.*

#### *The Collect.*

ALMIGHTY God, whom truly to know is everlasting life: grant us perfectly to know thy Son Jesus Christ, to be the way, the truth, and the life, as thou hast taught Saint Philip, and other the apostles: Through Jesus Christ our Lord.

*The Epistle.* James. i. James the servant of God, [&c.]
[i.e. James i. verse 1 to verse 13.]

*The Gospel.* John xiv. And Jesus said unto his disciples . . . . . [&c.]
[i.e. John xiv. verse 1 to verse 15.]

### *Saint Barnabe Apostle.*

#### *The Collect.*

LORD almighty, which hast endued thy holy Apostle Barnabas, with singular gifts of thy Holy Ghost: let us not be destitute of thy manifold gifts, nor yet of grace, to use them alway to thy honour and glory: Through Jesus Christ our Lord.

*The Epistle.* Act. xi. Tidings of these things came unto . . . . . [&c.]
[i.e. Act. xi. verse 22 to the end.]

*The Gospel.* John xv. This is my commandment that ye love together . . . . . [&c.]
[i.e. John xv. verse 12 to verse 17.]

### *Saint John Baptist.*

#### *The Collect.*

ALMIGHTY God, by whose providence thy servant John Baptist was wonderfully born, and sent to prepare the way of thy Son our Saviour by preaching of penance: make us so to follow his doctrine and holy life, that we may truly repent, according to his preaching, and after his example constantly speak the truth, boldly rebuke vice, and patiently suffer for the truth's sake: through Jesus Christ our Lord.

*The Epistle.* Esay. xl. Be of good cheer my people . . . . . [&c.]
[i.e. Isai. xl. verse 1 to verse 12.]

*The Gospel.* Luke. i. Elizabeth's time came... [&c.]
[i.e. Luke i. verse 57 to the end.]

### *Saint Peter's Day.*

#### *The Collect.*

ALMIGHTY God, which by thy Son Jesus Christ hast given to thy Apostle Saint Peter many excellent gifts, and commandest [a] him earnestly to feed thy flock: make, we beseech thee, all Bishops and Pastors diligently tò preach thy holy word, and the people obediently to follow the same, that they may receive the crown of everlasting glory: through Jesus Christ our Lord.

*The Epistle.* Acts xii. At the same time, Herod the King ..... [&c.]

[i.e. Acts xii. verse 1 to verse 12.]

*The Gospel.* Mat. xvi. When Jesus came into the coasts ..... [&c.]

[i.e. Mat. xvi. verse 13 to verse 20.]

### *Saint James the Apostle.*

#### *The Collect.*

GRANT, O merciful God, that as thy holy Apostle Saint James [t], leaving his father and all that he had, without delay, was obedient unto the calling of thy Son Jesus Christ, and followed him: So we, forsaking all worldly and carnal affections, may be evermore [u] ready to follow thy commandments: through Jesu Christ our Lord.

*The Epistle.* Acts xi. Acts xii. In those days came prophets from ..... [&c.]

[i.e. Acts xi. verse 27 to verse 3 of chap. xii.]

*The Gospel.* Math. xx. Then came to him the mother of Zebedee's children ..... [&c.]

[i.e. Matt. xx. verse 20 to verse 29.]

---

[a] In some copies, "commandest." [t] In some copies, "thy holy Apostle Saint James;" and in some copies, "thy holy Apostle James."
[u] In some copies, "may evermore be."

### Saint Bartholomew.

#### The Collect.

O ALMIGHTY and everlasting God, which hast given grace to thy Apostle Bartholomew truly to believe and to preach thy word: grant, we beseech thee, unto thy church, both to love that he believed, and to preach that he taught: through Christ our Lord.

*The Epistle.* Acts v. By the hands of the Apostles ..... [&c.]
[i.e. Acts v. verse 12 to verse 17.]

*The Gospel.* Luke xxii. And there was a strife among them ..... [&c.]
[i.e. Luke xxii. verse 24 to verse 31.]

### Saint Mathew.

#### The Collect.

ALMIGHTY God, which by thy blessed Son didst call Mathew from the receipt of custom to be an Apostle and Evangelist: Grant us grace to forsake all covetous desires, and inordinate love of riches, and to follow thy said Son Jesus Christ: who liveth and reigneth. &c.

*The Epistle.* 2 Cor. iv. Seeing that we have such an office ..... [&c.]
[i.e. 2 Cor. iv. verse 1 to verse 7.]

*The Gospel.* Math. ix. And as Jesus passed forth, [&c.]
[i.e. Matt. ix. verse 9 to verse 14.]

### Saint Michael and all Angels.

#### The Collect.

EVERLASTING God, which hast ordained and constituted the services of all Angels and men in a wonderful order: mercifully grant, that they which alway do thee service in heaven, may by thy appointment succour and defend us in earth: through Jesus Christ our Lord. &c.

*The Epistle.* Apoc. xii. There was a great battle in heaven . . . . . [&c.]
[i.e. Apoc. xii. verse 7 to verse 13.]

*The Gospel.* Mat. xviii. At the same time came the disciples . . . . . [&c.]
[i.e. Matt. xviii. verse 1 to verse 11.]

### *Saint Luke the Evangelist.*

#### *The Collect.*

ALMIGHTY God, which calledst Luke the physician, whose praise is in the gospel, to be a physician of the soul: it may please thee by the wholesome medicines of his doctrine to heal all the diseases of our souls: through thy Son Jesu Christ our Lord.

*The Epistle.* 2 Tim. iv. Watch thou in all things . . . . . [&c.]
[i.e. 2 Tim. iv. verse 5 to verse 16.]

*The Gospel.* Luke x. The Lord appointed other seventy . . . . . [&c.]
[i.e. Luke x. verse 1 to verse 7.]

### *Simon and Jude Apostles.*

#### *The Collect.*

ALMIGHTY GOD, which hast builded thy congregation upon the foundation of the Apostles and Prophets, Jesu Christ himself being the head corner stone: grant us so to be joined together in unity of spirit by their doctrine, that we may be made an holy temple acceptable to thee: through Jesu Christ our Lord[1].

*The Epistle.* Jude 1. Judas the servant of Jesus Christ . . . . . [&c.]
[i.e. Jude verse 1 to verse 9.]

*The Gospel.* John xv. This command I you . . [&c.]
[i.e. John xv. verse 17 to the end.]

### *All Saints.*

#### *The Collect.*

ALMIGHTY God, which hast knit together thy elect in one communion and fellowship, in the mystical body of thy Son Christ our Lord: grant us grace so to follow thy holy Saints in all virtues, and godly living, that we may come to those inspeakable joys, which thou hast prepared for them that unfeignedly love thee: Through Jesus Christ our Lord. Amen.

*The Epistle.* Apoca. vii. Behold, I John saw another angel . . . . . [&c.]
[i.e. Apoc. vii. verse 2 to verse 13.]

*The Gospel.* Math. v. Jesus seeing the people, [&c.]
[i.e. Matt. v. verse 1 to verse 13.]

---

[1] In some copies, "Amen" is added.

# THE ORDER FOR THE ADMINISTRATION OF THE LORD'S SUPPER, OR HOLY COMMUNION.

*SO many as intend to be partakers of the holy Communion, shall signify their names to the Curate over night, or else in the morning, afore the beginning of morning prayer, or immediately after.*

*And if any of those be an open and notorious evil liver, so that the congregation by him is offended, or have done any wrong to his neighbours, by word or deed: The Curate having knowledge thereof, shall call him, and advertise him, in any wise not to presume to the Lord's Table, until he have openly declared himself to have truly repented, and amended his former naughty life, that the congregation may thereby be satisfied, which afore were offended: and that he have recompensed the parties, whom he hath done wrong unto, or at the least declare himself to be in full purpose so to do, as soon as he conveniently may.*

*The same order shall the Curate use with those, betwixt whom he perceiveth malice and hatred to reign, not suffering them to be partakers of the LORD'S table, until he know them to be reconciled. And if one of the parties so at variance be content to forgive, from the bottom of his heart, all that the other hath trespassed against him, and to make amends for that he himself hath offended: and the other party will not be persuaded to a godly unity, but remain still in his frowardness and malice: The Minister in that case ought to admit the penitent person to the holy Communion, and not him that is obstinate.*

*The Table having at the Communion time a fair white linen cloth upon it, shall stand in the body of the Church, or in the chancel, where Morning prayer and Evening prayer be appointed to be said. And the priest standing at the north side of the Table, shall say the Lord's prayer, with this Collect following.*

ALMIGHTY God, unto whom all hearts be open, all desires known, and from whom no secrets are hid: cleanse the thoughts of our hearts by the inspiration of thy Holy Spirit, that we may perfectly love thee, and worthily magnify thy holy name: through Christ our Lord. Amen.

*Then shall the Priest rehearse distinctly all the Ten Commandments: and the people kneeling, shall after every Commandment ask God's mercy for their transgression of the same, after this sort.*

*Minister.*

God spake these words, and said: I am the Lord thy God. Thou shalt have none other gods but me.

*People.*

Lord, have mercy upon us, and incline our hearts to keep this law.

*Minister.*

Thou shalt not make to thyself any graven image, nor the likeness of any thing that is in heaven above, or in the earth beneath, or[y] in the water under the earth. Thou shalt not bow down to them, nor worship them: for I the Lord thy God am a jealous God, and visit the sin of the fathers upon the children, unto the third and fourth generation of them that hate me, and shew mercy unto thousands in them that love me and keep my commandments.

*People.*

Lord, have mercy upon us, and incline our hearts to keep this law.

*Minister.*

Thou shalt not take the name of the Lord thy God

---

[y] In some copies, " nor,"

in vain: for the Lord will not hold him guiltless that taketh his name in vain.

*People.*

Lord, have mercy upon us, and incline our. &c.

*Minister.*

Remember that thou keep holy the Sabbath day. Six days shalt thou labour and do all that thou hast to do, but the seventh day is the sabbath of the Lord thy God. In it thou shalt do no manner of work, thou and thy son and thy daughter, thy man servant, and thy maidservant, thy cattle, and the stranger that is within thy gates: for in six days the Lord made heaven and earth, the sea, and all that in them is, and rested the seventh day. Wherefore the Lord blessed the seventh day, and hallowed it.

*People.*

Lord, have mercy upon us, and incline our. &c.

*Minister.*

Honour thy father and thy mother, that thy days may be long in the land which the Lord thy God giveth thee.

*People.*

Lord, have mercy upon us, and incline our. &c.

*Minister.*

Thou shalt do no murther[1].

*People.*

Lord, have mercy upon us, and incline our. &c.

*Minister.*

Thou shalt not commit adultery.

*People.*

Lord, have mercy upon us, and incline our. &c.

*Minister.*

Thou shalt not steal.

*People.*

Lord, have mercy upon us, and incline our. &c.

---

[1] In some copies, "shalt not do murder."

*Minister.*

Thou shalt not bear false witness against thy neighbour.

*People.*

Lord, have mercy upon us, and incline our hearts to keep this law.

*Minister.*

Thou shalt not covet thy neighbour's house. Thou shalt not covet thy neighbour's wife, nor his servant, nor his maid, nor his ox, nor his ass, nor any thing that is his.

*People.*

Lord, have mercy upon us, and write all these thy laws in our hearts we beseech thee.

*Then shall follow the Collect of the day, with one of these two Collects following for the king: the Priest standing up and saying.*

Let us pray.

*Priest.*

ALMIGHTY God, whose kingdom is everlasting, and power infinite: have mercy upon the whole congregation, and so rule the heart of thy chosen servant Edward the sixth, our king and governor, that he (knowing whose minister he is) may above all things seek thy honour and glory: and that we his subjects (duly considering whose authority he hath) may faithfully serve, honour, and humbly obey him, in thee, and for thee, according to thy blessed word and ordinance: Through Jesus Christ our Lord, who with thee, and the Holy Ghost, liveth, and reigneth ever one God, world without end. Amen.

ALMIGHTY and everlasting God, we be taught by thy holy word, that the hearts of kings are in thy rule and governance, and that thou dost dispose, and turn them as it seemeth best to thy godly wisdom: we humbly beseech thee, so to dispose and govern the heart of Edward the sixth, thy servant, our king and governor, that in all his thoughts, words, and works, he may ever seek thy honour and glory, and study to preserve thy people committed to his charge, in wealth, peace, and godliness. Grant this, O merciful Father, for thy dear Son's sake Jesus Christ our Lord. Amen.

*Immediately after the Collects, the Priest shall read the Epistle, beginning thus.*

The Epistle written in the.     Chapter of.

*And the Epistle ended, he shall say the Gospel, beginning thus.*

The Gospel, written in the.     Chapter of.

*And the Epistle and Gospel being ended, shall be said the Creed.*

I BELIEVE in one God, the Father almighty, maker of heaven and earth, and of all things visible, and invisible: And in one Lord Jesu Christ, the only begotten Son of God, begotten[a] of his Father before all worlds: God of God[b], light of light, very God of very God: begotten, not made, being of one substance with the Father, by whom all things were made: who for us men and for our salvation, came down from heaven, and was incarnate by the Holy Ghost, of the virgin Mary, and was made man: and was crucified also for us, under Pontius Pilate. He suffered and was buried, and the third day he rose again according to the scriptures: and ascended into heaven, and sitteth at the right hand of the Father. And he shall come again with glory, to judge both the quick and the dead: Whose kingdom shall have none end. And I believe in the Holy Ghost, the Lord and giver of life, who proceedeth from the Father and the Son, who with the Father and the Son together, is wor-

---

[a] In some copies, "gotten."     [b] In some copies, "God of Gods."

shipped and glorified, who spake by the Prophets. And I believe one Catholic and Apostolic church. I acknowledge one Baptism, for the remission of sins. And I look for the resurrection of the dead, and the life of the world to come. Amen.

*After the Creed, if there be no sermon, shall follow one of the homilies already set forth, or hereafter to be set forth by common authority.*

*After such sermon, homily, or exhortation, the Curate shall declare unto the people whether there be any holy days or fasting days the week following: and earnestly exhort them to remember the poor, saying one or more of these Sentences following, as he thinketh most convenient by his discretion.*

LET your light so shine before men, that they may see your good works, and glorify your Father which is in heaven. *Math.* v.

Lay not up for yourselves treasure upon the earth, where the rust and moth doth corrupt, and where thieves break through and steal: But lay up for yourselves treasure in heaven, where neither rust nor moth doth corrupt, and where thieves do not break through and steal. *Math.* vi.

Whatsoever you would that men should do unto you, even so do unto them: for this is the law and the Prophets. *Math.* vii.

Not every one that saith unto me, Lord, Lord, shall enter into the kingdom of heaven, but he that doeth the will of my Father which is in heaven. *Math.* vii.

Zache stood forth, and said unto the Lord, Behold, Lord, the half of my goods I give to the poor, and if I have done any wrong to any man, I restore fourfold. *Luk.* xix.

Who goeth a warfare at any time at his own cost? Who planteth a vineyard, and eateth not of the fruit thereof? Or who feedeth a flock, and eateth not of the milk of the flock? 1 *Cor.* ix.

If we have sown unto you spiritual things, is it a great matter if we shall reap your worldly things? 1 *Cor.* ix.

Do ye not know, that they which minister about holy things, live of the sacrifice? They which wait of the altar are partakers with the altar? Even so hath the Lord also ordained: that they which preach the Gospel, should live of the Gospel. 1 *Cor.* ix.

He which soweth little, shall reap little, and he that soweth plenteously, shall reap plenteously. Let every man do according as he is disposed in his heart; not grudgingly [c], or of necessity; for God loveth a cheerful giver. 2 *Cor.* ix.

Let him that is taught in the word, minister unto him that teacheth, in all good things. Be not deceived; God is not mocked. For whatsoever a man soweth, that shall he reap. *Gala.* vi.

While we have time, let us do good unto all men, and specially unto them, which are of the household of faith. *Gala.* vi.

Godliness is great riches, if a man be contented [d] with that he hath: For we brought nothing into the world, neither may we carry any thing out. 1 *Tim.* vi.

Charge them which are rich in this world, that they be ready to give, and glad to distribute, laying up in store for themselves a good foundation, against the time to come, that they may attain eternal life. 1 *Tim.* vi.

God is not unrighteous, that he will forget your works and labour, that proceedeth of love, which love ye have shewed for his name's sake, which have ministered unto the saints, and yet do minister. *Hebre.* vi.

To do good, and to distribute, forget not, for with such sacrifices God is pleased. *Hebr.* xiii.

Whoso hath this world's good, and seeth his brother have need, and shutteth up his compassion

---

[c] In some copies, "grudging"   [d] In some copies, "content."

from him, how dwelleth the love of God in him? 1 *John* iii.

Give alms of thy goods, and turn never thy face from any poor man, and then the face of the Lord shall not be turned away from thee. *Tob.* iv.

Be merciful after thy power. If thou hast much, give plenteously: If thou hast little, do thy diligence gladly to give of that little: for so gatherest thou thyself a good reward in the day of necessity. *Tob.* iv.

He that hath pity upon the poor lendeth unto the Lord; and look, what he layeth out, it shall be paid him again. *Prov.* xix.

Blessed be the man that provideth for the sick and needy; the Lord shall deliver him, in the time of trouble. *Psalm* xli.

*Then shall the Church wardens, or some other by them appointed, gather the devotion of the people, and put the same into the poor men's box: and upon the offering days appointed, every man and woman shall pay to the Curate the due and accustomed offerings: after which done the Priest shall say.*

Let us pray for the whole state of Christ's Church militant here in earth.

ALMIGHTY and everliving God, which by thy holy apostle hast taught us to make prayers and supplications, and to give thanks for all men: We humbly beseech thee most mercifully to accept our\* alms and to receive these our prayers, which we offer unto thy divine Majesty, beseeching thee to inspire continually the universal church with the spirit of truth, unity, and concord: And grant that all they that do confess thy holy name, may agree in the truth of thy holy word, and live in unity and godly love. We beseech thee also to save and defend all Christian Kings, Princes, and Governours, and specially thy servant, Edward our King,

\* If there be none alms given unto the poor, then shall the words of accepting our alms be left out unsaid.

that under him we may be godly and quietly governed: and grant unto his whole council, and to all that be put in authority under him, that they may truly and indifferently minister justice, to the punishment of wickedness and vice, and to the maintenance of God's true religion and virtue. Give grace (O heavenly Father) to all Bishops, Pastors, and Curates, that they may both by their life and doctrine set forth thy true and lively word, and rightly and duly administer thy holy Sacraments: and to all thy people give thy heavenly grace, and especially to this congregation here present, that with meek heart and due reverence they may hear and receive thy holy word, truly serving thee in holiness and righteousness all the days of their life. And we most humbly beseech thee of thy goodness (O Lord) to comfort and succour all them, which in this transitory life be in trouble, sorrow, need, sickness, or any other adversity: Grant this, O Father, for Jesus Christ's sake, our only Mediator and Advocate. Amen.

*Then shall follow this exhortation at certain times when the Curate shall see the people negligent to come to the holy Communion.*

WE be come together at this time, dearly beloved brethren, to feed at the Lord's supper, unto the which in God's behalf I bid you all that be here present, and beseech you for the Lord Jesus Christ's sake, that ye will not refuse to come thereto, being so lovingly called and bidden of God himself. Ye know how grievous and unkind a thing it is, when a man hath prepared a rich feast, decked his table with all kind of provision, so that there lacketh nothing but the guests to sit down: and yet they which be called, without any cause most unthankfully refuse to come. Which of you, in such a case, would not be moved? Who would not think a great injury and wrong done unto him? Wherefore, most dearly beloved in Christ, take ye good heed, lest ye withdrawing yourselves from this holy supper, provoke God's indignation against you. It is an easy matter for a man to say, I will not communicate, because I am otherwise letted with worldly business: but such excuses be not so easily accepted and allowed before God. If any man say, I am a grievous sinner, and therefore am afraid to come: wherefore then do you not repent and amend? When God calleth you, be you not ashamed to say you will not come? When you should return to God, will you excuse yourself and say that you be not ready? Consider earnestly with yourselves how little such feigned excuses shall avail before God. They that refused the feast in the gospel, because they had bought a farm, or would try their yokes of oxen, or because they were married, were not so excused, but counted unworthy of the heavenly feast. I for my part am here present, and according to mine office, I bid you in the name of God, I call you in Christ's behalf, I exhort you, as you love your own salvation, that ye will be partakers of this holy Communion. And as the Son of God did vouchsafe to yield up his soul by death upon the Cross for your health: even so it is your duty to receive the Communion together in the remembrance of his death, as he himself commanded. Now if you will in no wise thus do, consider with yourselves how great injury you do unto God, and how sore punishment hangeth over your heads for the same. And whereas ye offend God so sore in refusing this holy Banquet, I admonish, exhort, and beseech you, that unto this unkindness ye will not add any more. Which thing ye shall do, if ye stand by as gazers and lookers on them that do communicate, and be no partakers of the same yourselves. For what thing can this be accounted else, than a further contempt and unkindness unto God. Truly it is a great unthankfulness to say nay when ye be called: but the fault is much greater when men stand by, and yet will neither eat nor drink this holy Communion with other. I pray you what can this be else, but even to have the mysteries of Christ in derision? It is said unto all: Take ye and eat. Take and drink ye all of this: do this in remembrance of me. With what face then, or with what countenance shall ye hear these words? What will this be else but a neglecting, a despising, and mocking of the Testament of Christ? Wherefore, rather than you should so do, depart you hence and give place to them that be godly disposed. But when you depart, I beseech you, ponder with yourselves from whom you depart: ye depart from the Lord's table, ye depart from your brethren, and from the banquet of most heavenly food. These things if ye earnestly consider, ye shall by God's grace return to a better mind, for the obtaining whereof, we shall make our humble petitions while we shall receive the holy Communion.

*And sometime shall be said this also, at the discretion of the Curate.*

DEARLY beloved, forasmuch as our duty is to render to Almighty God our heavenly Father most hearty thanks, for that he hath given his Son our Saviour Jesus Christ, not only to die for us, but also to be our spiritual food and sustenance, as it is declared unto us, as well by God's word as by the holy Sacraments of his blessed body and blood, the which being so comfortable a thing to them which receive it worthily, and so dangerous to them that will presume to receive it unworthily: My duty is to exhort you to consider the dignity of the holy mystery, and the great peril of the unworthy receiving thereof, and so to search and examine your own consciences, as you should come holy and clean to a most Godly and heavenly feast: so that in no wise you come but in the marriage garment, required of God in holy scripture; and so come and be received, as worthy partakers of such a heavenly table. The way and means thereto is: First to examine your lives and conversation by the rule of God's commandments, and wheresoever ye shall perceive yourselves to have offended, either by will, word, or deed, there bewail your own sinful lives, confess yourselves to almighty God with full purpose of amendment of life. And if ye shall perceive your offences to be such, as be not only against God, but also against your neighbours: then ye shall reconcile yourselves unto them, ready to make restitution and satisfaction, according to the uttermost of your powers, for all injuries and wrongs done by you to any other: and likewise being ready to forgive other that have offended you, as you would have forgiveness of your offences at God's hand: for otherwise the receiving of the holy Communion doth nothing else, but increase your damnation. And because it is requisite that no man should come to the holy Communion but with a full trust in God's mercy, and with a quiet conscience: therefore if there be any of you which by the means afore said cannot quiet his own conscience, but requireth further comfort or counsel; then let him come to me, or some other discreet and learned minister of God's word, and open his grief, that he may receive such ghostly counsel, advice, and comfort, as his conscience may be relieved; and that by the ministery of God's word he may receive comfort and the benefit of absolution, to the quieting of his conscience, and avoiding of all scruple and doubtfulness.

¶ *Then shall the Priest say this exhortation.*

DEARLY beloved in the Lord: ye that mind to come to the holy Communion of the body and blood of our Saviour Christ, must consider what St. Paul writeth to the Corinthians, how he exhorteth all persons diligently to try and examine themselves, before they presume to eat of that bread, and drink of that cup: for as the benefit is great, if with a truly penitent heart and lively faith, we receive that holy Sacrament, (for then we spiritually eat the flesh of Christ, and drink his blood, then we dwell in Christ and Christ in us, we be one with Christ, and Christ with us;) so is the danger great, if we receive the same unworthily. For then we be guilty of the body and blood of Christ our Saviour. We eat and drink our own damnation, not considering the Lord's body. We kindle God's wrath against us, we provoke him to plague us with divers diseases, and sundry kinds of death. Therefore, if any of you be a blasphemer of God, an hinderer or slanderer of his word, an adulterer, or be in malice or envy, or in any other grievous crime, bewail your sins, and come not to this holy Table; lest after the taking of that holy Sacrament, the Devil enter into you, as he entered into Judas, and fill you full of all iniquities, and bring you to destruction, both of body and soul. Judge therefore yourselves (brethren) that ye be not judged of the Lord. Repent you truly for your sins past, have a lively and stedfast faith in Christ our Saviour. Amend your lives, and be in perfect charity with all men, so shall ye be meet partakers of those holy mysteries. And above all things, ye must give most humble and hearty thanks to God the Father, the Son, and the Holy Ghost, for the redemption of the world by the death and passion of our Saviour Christ, both God and man, who did humble himself, even to the death upon the Cross, for us miserable sinners, which lay in darkness and shadow of death, that he might make us the children of God, and exalt us to everlasting life. And to the end that we should alway remember the exceeding great love of our Master, and only Saviour Jesu Christ, thus dying for us, and the innumerable benefits, (which by his precious blood-shedding) he hath obtained to us, he hath instituted and ordained holy mysteries, as pledges of his love, and continual remembrance of his death, to our great and endless comfort. To him therefore, with the Father and the Holy Ghost, let us give (as we are most bounden) continual thanks: submitting ourselves wholly to his holy will and pleasure, and studying to serve him in true holiness and righteousness, all the days of our life. Amen.

*Then shall the Priest say to those that come to receive the holy Communion.*

YOU that do truly and earnestly repent you of your sins, and be in love and charity with your neighbours, and intend to lead a new life, following the commandments of God, and walking from henceforth in his holy ways: Draw near and take this holy Sacrament to your comfort: make your humble confession to Almighty God, before this congregation here gathered together in his holy name, meekly kneeling upon your knees.

*Then shall this general confession be made, in the name of all those that are minded to receive the holy Communion, either by one of them, or else by one of the ministers, or by the Priest himself, all kneeling humbly upon their knees.*

ALMIGHTY God, Father of our Lord Jesus Christ, maker of all things, Judge of all men, we acknowledge [a] and bewail our manifold sins and wickedness, which we from time to time most grievously have committed, by thought, word and deed, against thy divine Majesty: provoking most justly thy wrath and indignation against us: we do earnestly repent, and be heartily sorry for these our misdoings: the remembrance of them is grievous unto us, the burthen of them is intolerable: have mercy upon us, have mercy upon us,

---

[a] In several copies, "knowledge."

## THE COMMUNION.               79

most merciful Father, for thy Son our Lord Jesus Christ's sake: forgive us all that is past, and grant that we may ever hereafter serve and please thee, in newness of life, to the honour and glory of thy name: Through Jesus Christ our Lord.

¶ *Then shall the Priest or the Bishop (being present) stand up, and turning himself to the people,* †*say thus,*

ALMIGHTY God, our heavenly Father, who of his great mercy, hath promised forgiveness of sins to all them, which with hearty repentance and true faith turn unto him: have mercy upon you, pardon and déliver you from all your sins, confirm and strengthen you in all goodness, and bring you to everlasting life: through Jesus Christ our Lord.   Amen.

¶ *Then shall the Priest also say,*

Hear what comfortable words our Saviour Christ saith, to all that truly turn to him.

Come unto me all that travail, and be heavy laden, and I shall refresh you.  So GOD loved the world, that he gave his only begotten Son, to the end that all that believe in him, should not perish, but have life everlasting.

Hear also what Saint Paul sayeth.

This is a true saying, and worthy of all men to be received, that Jesus Christ came into this world to save sinners.

Hear also what Saint John sayeth.

If any man sin, we have an advocate with the Father, Jesus Christ the righteous, and he is the propitiation for our sins.

¶ *After the which, the Priest shall proceed, saying,*

Lift up your hearts.
*Answer.* We lift them up unto the Lord.

† In some copies, "shall say."

*Priest.* Let us give thanks unto our Lord God.
*Answer.* It is meet and right so to do.
*Priest.* It is very meet, right, and our bounden duty, that we should at all times, and in all places, give thanks unto thee, O Lord holy Father, almighty everlasting God.

*Here shall follow the proper preface* [g] *according to the time (if there be any specially appointed,) or else immediately shall follow,* Therefore with Angels, &c.

## PROPER PREFACES.

*Upon Christmas day, and seven days after.*

BECAUSE thou didst give Jesus Christ, thine only Son, to be born as this day for us, who by the operation of the Holy Ghost, was made very man, of the substance of the Virgin Mary his mother, and that without spot of sin, to make us clean from all sin. Therefore. &c.

*Upon Easter day, and seven days after.*

BUT chiefly are we bound to praise thee, for the glorious resurrection of Thy Son Jesus Christ our Lord; for he is the very Paschal Lamb, which was offered for us, and hath taken away the sin of the world, who by his death hath destroyed death, and by his rising to life again hath restored to us everlasting life. Therefore. &c.

*Upon the Ascension day, and seven days after.*

THROUGH thy most dear beloved Son, Jesus Christ our Lord, who after his most glorious resurrection manifestly appeared to all his Apostles, and in their sight ascended up into heaven, to prepare a place for us, that where he is, thither might we also ascend, and reign with him in glory. Therefore with Angels. &c.

[g] In some copies, "Prefaces."

### Upon Whitsunday, and six days after.

THROUGH Jesus Christ our Lord, according to whose most true promise, the Holy Ghost came down this day from heaven, with a sudden great sound, as it had been a mighty wind, in the likeness of fiery tongues, lighting upon the Apostles, to teach them, and to lead them to all truth, giving them both the gift of divers languages, and also boldness with fervent zeal, constantly to preach the Gospel unto all nations, whereby we are brought out of darkness and error, into the clear light and true knowledge of thee, and of thy Son Jesus Christ. Therefore with. &c.

### Upon the feast of Trinity only.

IT is very meet, right, and our bounden duty, that we should at all times, and in all places, give thanks to thee, O Lord, almighty and everlasting God, which art one God, one Lord, not one only person, but three persons in one substance: For that which we believe of the glory of the Father, the same we believe of the Son, and of the Holy Ghost, without any difference, or inequality. Therefore with. &c.

*After which preface, shall follow immediately,*

Therefore with Angels and Archangels, and with all the company of heaven, we laud and magnify thy glorious name, evermore praising thee, and saying:

Holy, holy, holy, Lord God of Hosts: heaven and earth are full of thy glory: glory be to thee, O Lord, most high.

*Then shall the Priest, kneeling down at God's board, say in the name of all them that shall receive the Communion, this prayer following.*

WE do not presume to come to this thy table (O merciful Lord) trusting in our own righteousness, but in thy manifold and great mercies: we be not worthy so much as to gather up the crumbs under thy table: but thou art the same Lord whose property is always to have mercy: grant us therefore (gracious Lord) so to eat the flesh of thy dear Son Jesus Christ, and to drink his blood, that our sinful bodies may be made clean by his body, and our souls washed through his most precious blood, and that we may evermore dwell in him, and he in us. Amen

*Then the Priest standing up shall say, as followeth.*

ALMIGHTY God our heavenly Father, which of thy tender mercy didst give thine only Son Jesus Christ, to suffer death upon the cross for our redemption, who made there (by his one oblation of himself once offered) a full, perfect and sufficient sacrifice, oblation, and satisfaction, for the sins of the whole world, and did institute, and in his holy Gospel command us to continue, a perpetual memory of that his precious death, until his coming again: Hear us O merciful Father we beseech thee; and grant that we, receiving these thy creatures of bread and wine, according to thy Son our Saviour Jesus Christ's holy institution, in remembrance of his death and passion, may be partakers of his most blessed body and blood: who, in the same night that he was betrayed, took bread, and when he had given thanks, he brake it, and gave it to his disciples, saying: Take, eat, this is my body which is given for you. Do this in remembrance of me. Likewise after supper he took the cup, and when he had given thanks, he gave it to them, saying: Drink ye all of this, for this is my blood of the new Testament, which is shed for you and for many, for remission of sins: do this as oft as ye shall drink it in remembrance of me.

*Then shall the minister first receive the Communion in both kinds himself, and next deliver it to other ministers,*

## THE COMMUNION. 83

*if any be there present (that they may help the chief minister,) and after to the people in their hands kneeling.*
*And when he delivereth the bread, he shall say.*

Take and eat this, in remembrance that Christ died for thee, and feed on him in thy heart by faith, with thanksgiving.

*And the Minister that delivereth the cup, shall say,*

Drink this in remembrance that Christ's blood was shed for thee, and be thankful.

*Then shall the Priest say the Lord's prayer, the people repeating after him every petition.*
*After shall be said as followeth.*

O LORD and heavenly Father, we thy humble servants, entirely desire thy fatherly goodness, mercifully to accept this our Sacrifice of praise and thanksgiving: most humbly beseeching thee to grant, that by the merits and death of thy Son Jesus Christ, and through faith in his blood, we and all thy whole church may obtain remission of our sins, and all other benefits of his passion. And here we offer and present unto thee, O Lord, ourselves, our souls, and bodies, to be a reasonable, holy, and lively sacrifice unto thee: humbly beseeching thee, that all we which be partakers of this holy Communion, may be fulfilled with thy grace and heavenly benediction. And although we be unworthy through our manifold sins to offer unto thee any Sacrifice: yet we beseech thee to accept this our bounden duty and service, not weighing our merits, but pardoning our offences, through Jesus Christ our Lord; by whom and with whom, in the unity of the Holy Ghost, all honour and glory be unto thee, O Father Almighty, world without end. Amen.

*Or this.*

ALMIGHTY and everliving God, we most heartily thank thee, for that thou dost vouchsafe to feed us, which have duly received these holy mysteries, with the spiritual food of the most precious body and blood of thy Son our Saviour Jesus Christ, and dost assure us thereby of thy favour and goodness toward us, and that we be very members incorporate in thy mystical body, which is the blessed company of all faithful people, and be also heirs through hope of thy everlasting kingdom, by the merits of the most precious death and passion of thy dear Son. We now most humbly beseech thee, O heavenly Father, so to assist us with thy grace, that we may continue in that holy fellowship, and do all such good works, as thou hast prepared for us to walk in: through Jesus Christ our Lord, to whom, with thee and the Holy Ghost, be all honour and glory, world without end. Amen.

*Then shall be said or sung.*

GLORY be to God on high. And in earth peace, good will towards men. We praise thee, we bless thee, we worship thee, we glorify thee, we give thanks to thee for thy great glory, O Lord God heavenly king, God the Father almighty. O Lord the only begotten Son Jesu Christ: O Lord God, Lamb of God, son of the Father, that takest away the sins of the world, have mercy upon us: Thou that takest away the sins of the world, have mercy upon us. Thou that takest away the sins of the world, receive our prayer. Thou that sittest at the right hand of God the Father, have mercy upon us: For thou only art holy, Thou only art the Lord. Thou only, O Christ, with the Holy Ghost, art most high in the glory of God the Father. Amen.

*Then the Priest or the Bishop, if he be present, shall let them depart with this blessing:*

The peace of GOD (which passeth all understanding) keep your hearts and minds in the knowledge and love of GOD, and of his Son Jesus Christ our Lord: And the blessing of God Almighty, the Father, the Son, and the Holy Ghost, be amongst you and remain with you always. Amen.

*Collects to be said after the Offertory, when there is no Communion, every such day one. And the same may be said also as often as occasion shall serve, after the Collects, either of Morning and Evening prayer, Communion or Litany, by the discretion of the minister.*

ASSIST us mercifully, O Lord, in these our supplications and prayers, and dispose the way of thy servants toward the attainment of everlasting salvation: that among all the changes and chances of this mortal life, they may ever be defended by thy most gracious and ready help: through Christ our Lord. Amen.

O ALMIGHTY Lord and everliving God, vouchsafe, we beseech thee, to direct, sanctify, and govern, both our hearts and bodies, in the ways of thy laws, and in the works of thy commandments: that through thy most mighty protection, both here and ever, we may be preserved in body and soul: through our Lord and Saviour Jesus Christ. Amen.

GRANT, we beseech thee, Almighty God, that the words which we have heard this day, with our outward ears, may through thy grace be so grafted inwardly in our hearts, that they may bring forth in us the fruit of good living, to the honour and praise of thy name: through Jesus Christ our Lord. Amen.

PREVENT us, O Lord, in all our doings, with thy most gracious favour, and further us with thy continual help, that in all our works begun, continued, and ended in thee, we may glorify thy holy name, and finally by thy mercy obtain everlasting life: through Jesus Christ our Lord. Amen.

ALMIGHTY God, the fountain of all wisdom, which knowest our necessities before we ask, and our ignorance in asking: we beseech thee to have compassion upon our infirmities, and those things, which for our unworthiness we dare not, and for our blindness we cannot ask, vouchsafe to give us for the worthiness of thy Son Jesus Christ our Lord. Amen.

ALMIGHTY God, which hast promised to hear the petitions of them that ask in thy Son's name: we beseech thee mercifully to incline thine ears to us that have made now our prayers and supplications unto thee: and grant that those things which we have faithfully asked according to thy will, may effectually be obtained to the relief of our necessity, and to the setting forth of thy glory: Through Jesus Christ our Lord. Amen.

*Upon the holy days, if there be no Communion, shall be said all that is appointed at the Communion, until the end of the Homily, concluding with the general prayer, 'for the whole state of Christ's Church militant here in earth:' and one or more of these Collects before rehearsed, as occasion shall serve.*

*And there shall be no celebration of the Lord's Supper, except there be a good number to communicate with the Priest, according to his discretion.*

*And if there be not above twenty persons in the Parish, of discretion to receive the Communion: yet there shall be no Communion, except four, or three at the least communicate with the Priest. And in Cathedral and Collegiate churches, where be many Priests and Deacons, they shall all receive the Communion with the minister every Sunday at the least, except they have a reasonable cause to the contrary.*

*And to take away the superstition, which any person hath, or might have in the bread and wine, it shall suffice that the bread be such, as is usual to be eaten at the table with other meats, but the best and purest wheat bread, that conveniently may be gotten. And if any of the bread or wine remain, the Curate shall have it to his own use.*

*The bread and wine for the Communion shall be provided by the Curate, and the churchwardens, at the charges of the Parish, and the Parish shall be discharged of such sums of money, or other duties, which hitherto they have paid for the same, by order of their houses every Sunday.*

*And note, that every Parishioner shall communicate, at the least three times in the year: of which, Easter to be one: and shall also receive the Sacraments, and other rites, according to the order in this book appointed. And yearly at Easter, every Parishioner shall reckon with his Parson, Vicar, or Curate, or his, or their deputy or deputies, and pay to them or him all ecclesiastical duties, accustomably due, then and at that time to be paid.*

*Although no order can be so perfectly devised, but it may be of some, either for their ignorance and infirmity, or else of malice and obstinacy, misconstrued, depraved, and interpreted in a wrong part: And yet because brotherly charity willeth, that so much as conveniently may be, offences should be taken away: therefore we willing to do the same. Whereas it is ordained in the book of common prayer, in the administration of the Lord's Supper, that the Communicants kneeling should receive the holy Communion: which thing being well meant, for a signification of the humble and grateful acknowledging of the benefits of Christ, given unto the worthy receiver, and to avoid the profanation and disorder, which about the holy Communion might else ensue: lest yet the same kneeling might be thought or taken otherwise, we do declare that it is not meant thereby, that any adoration is done, or ought to be done, either unto the sacramental bread or wine there bodily received, or to any real and essential presence there being of Christ's natural flesh and blood. For as concerning the sacramental bread and wine, they remain still in their very natural substances, and therefore may not be adored, for that were Idolatry to be abhorred of all faithful Christians. And as concerning the natural body and blood of our Saviour Christ, they are in heaven and not here. For it is against the truth of Christ's true natural body, to be in more places than in one at one time.*

# THE MINISTRATION OF BAPTISM
## TO BE USED IN THE CHURCH.

*It appeareth by ancient writers, that the Sacrament of Baptism in the old time was not commonly ministered but at two times in the year: at Easter and Whitsuntide. At which times it was openly ministered in the presence of all the congregation: which custom (now being grown out of use) although it cannot for many considerations be well restored again, yet it is thought good to follow the same as near as conveniently may be: wherefore the people are to be admonished, that it is most convenient that Baptism should not be ministered but upon Sundays, and other holy days, when the most number of people may come together, as well for that the congregation there present may testify the receiving of them, that be newly baptized, into the number of Christ's Church, as also because in the Baptism of infants, every man present may be put in remembrance of his own profession made to God in his Baptism. For which cause also, it is expedient that Baptism be ministered in the English tongue. Nevertheless (if necessity so require) children may at all times be Baptized at home.*

## PUBLIC BAPTISM.

*When there are children to be baptized upon the Sunday or holy day, the Parents shall give knowledge over night or in the morning, afore the beginning of Morning prayer, to the Curate. And then the Godfathers, Godmothers, and people, with the children, must be ready at the Font, either immediately after the last Lesson at Morning prayer, or else immediately after the last Lesson at Evening prayer, as the Curate by his discretion shall appoint. And then standing there, the Priest shall ask whether the children be baptized or no. If they answer, no: then shall the Priest say thus.*

DEARLY beloved, forasmuch as all men be conceived and born in sin, and that our Saviour Christ saith, none can enter into the kingdom of God except he be regenerate and born anew of water and the Holy Ghost; I beseech you to call upon God the Father through our Lord Jesus Christ, that of his bounteous mercy, he will grant to these children, that thing which by nature they cannot have, that they may be baptized with water and the Holy Ghost, and received into Christ's holy church, and be made lively members of the same.

*Then the Priest shall say,*
Let us pray.

ALMIGHTY and everlasting God, which of thy great mercy didst save Noe and his family in the Ark from perishing by water: and also didst safely lead the children of Israel, thy people through the Red Sea: figuring thereby thy holy Baptism: and by the Baptism of thy wellbeloved Son Jesus Christ, didst sanctify the flood Jordan, and all other waters, to the mystical washing away of sin: We beseech thee for thy infinite mercies, that thou wilt mercifully look upon these children, sanctify them and wash them with thy Holy Ghost, that they, being delivered from thy wrath, may be received into the Ark of Christ's Church, and being steadfast in faith, joyful through hope, and rooted in charity, may so pass the waves of this troublesome world, that finally they may come to the land of everlasting life, there to reign with thee, world without end: through Jesus Christ our Lord. Amen.

ALMIGHTY and immortal God, the aid of all that need, the helper of all that flee to thee for succour, the life of them that believe, and the resurrection of the dead: We call upon thee for these infants, that they coming to thy holy Baptism, may receive remission of their sins by spiritual regeneration. Receive them (O Lord) as thou hast promised by thy well beloved Son, saying: Ask and you shall have, seek, and you shall find, knock, and it shall be opened unto you. So give now unto us that ask. Let us that seek find. Open the gate upon us that knock, that these infants may enjoy the everlasting benediction of thy heavenly washing, and may come to the eternal kingdom, which thou hast promised by Christ our Lord. Amen.

*Then shall the Priest say: Hear the words of the Gospel, written by Saint Mark in the tenth Chapter.*

At a certain time they brought children to Christ that he should touch them, and his disciples rebuked those that brought them. But when Jesus saw it, he was displeased, and said unto them: Suffer little children to come unto me, and forbid them not; for to such belongeth the kingdom of God. Verily I say unto you: whosoever doth not receive the kingdom of God, as a little child, he shall not enter therein. And when he had taken them up in his arms, he put his hands upon them, and blessed them.   Mark x.

*After the Gospel is read, the Minister shall make this brief exhortation upon the words of the Gospel.*

FRIENDS, you[h] hear in this Gospel the words of our Saviour Christ, that he commanded the children to be brought unto him: how he blamed those that would have kept them from him: how he exhorteth[i] all men to follow their innocency. Ye[k] perceive how by his outward gesture and deed he declared his good will toward them. For he embraced them in his arms, he laid his hands upon them, and blessed them. Doubt not ye[l] therefore, but earnestly believe, that he will likewise favourably receive these present infants, that he will embrace them with the arms of his mercy, that he will give unto them the blessing of eternal

---

[h] In some copies, "ye."
[k] In some copies, "You."
[i] In some copies, "exhorted."
[l] In some copies, "doubt not you."

life, and make them partakers of his everlasting kingdom. Wherefore we being thus persuaded of the good will of our heavenly Father toward these infants, declared by his Son Jesus Christ; and nothing doubting but that he favourably alloweth this charitable work of ours, in bringing these children to his holy Baptism: let us faithfully and devoutly give thanks unto him, and say.

ALMIGHTY and everlasting God, heavenly Father, we give thee humble thanks, that thou hast vouchsafed[m] to call us to the knowledge of thy grace, and faith in thee: increase this knowledge, and confirm this faith in us evermore: Give thy Holy Spirit to these infants, that they may be born again, and be made heirs of everlasting salvation, through our Lord Jesus Christ: who liveth and reigneth with thee and the Holy Spirit, now and for ever. Amen.

*Then the Priest shall speak unto the Godfathers and Godmothers, on this wise.*

Wellbeloved friends, ye have brought these children here to be baptized; ye have prayed that our Lord Jesus Christ would vouchsafe to receive them, to lay his hands upon them, to bless them, to release them of their sins, to give them the kingdom of heaven, and everlasting life. Ye have heard also that our Lord Jesus Christ hath promised in his Gospel, to grant all these things that ye have prayed for: which promise he for his part will most surely keep and perform. Wherefore after this promise made by Christ, these infants must also faithfully for their part promise by you that be their sureties, that they will forsake the devil and all his works, and constantly believe God's holy word, and obediently keep his commandments.

[m] In some copies, "vouchsafe."

*Then shall the Priest demand of the Godfathers and God-mothers these questions following*[n] :

Dost thou forsake the devil and all his works, the vain pomp and glory of the world, with all the[o] covetous desires of the same, the[p] carnal desires of the flesh, so that thou wilt not follow, nor be led by them?

*Answer.* I forsake them all.

*Minister.* Dost thou believe in God the Father Almighty, maker of heaven and earth? and in Jesus Christ his only begotten Son our Lord, and that he was conceived by the Holy Ghost, born of the virgin Mary, that he suffered under Poncius Pilate, was crucified, dead, and buried, that he went down into hell, and also did rise again the third day; that he ascended into heaven, and sitteth at the right hand of God the Father Almighty, and from thence shall come again at the end of the world, to judge the quick and the dead:

And dost thou believe in the Holy Ghost, the holy Catholic Church, the Communion of Saints, the remission of sins, the resurrection of the flesh, and everlasting life after death?

*Answer.* All this I steadfastly believe.

*Minister.* Wilt thou be baptized in this faith?

*Answer.* That is my desire.

*Then shall the Priest say.*

O MERCIFUL God, grant that the old Adam in these children may be so buried, that the new man may be raised up in them. Amen.

Grant that all carnal affections may die in them, and that all things belonging to the Spirit may live and grow in them. Amen.

Grant that they may have power and strength to have victory and to triumph against the devil, the world and the flesh. Amen.

---

[n] In some copies, "following" *omitted.*   [o] In some copies, "the" *omitted.*   [p] In some copies, "and the carnal."

Grant that whosoever is here dedicated to thee by our office and ministry, may also be endued with heavenly virtues, and everlastingly rewarded through thy mercy, O blessed Lord God, who dost live and govern all things world without end. Amen.

ALMIGHTY everliving God, whose most dearly beloved Son Jesus Christ, for the forgiveness of our sins, did shed out of his most precious side both water and blood, and gave commandment to his disciples that they should go teach all nations, and baptize them in the name of the Father, the Son, and of the Holy Ghost: Regard, we beseech thee, the supplications of thy congregation, and grant that all thy servants which shall be baptized in this water, may receive the fulness of thy grace, and ever remain in the number of thy faithful and elect children, through Jesus Christ our Lord. Amen.

*Then the Priest shall take the child in his hands, and ask the name: and naming the child, shall dip it in the water, so it be discreetly and warily done, saying.*

*N.* I baptize thee in the name of the Father, and of the Son, and of the Holy Ghost. Amen.

*And if the child be weak, it shall suffice to pour water upon it, saying the foresaid words.*

*N.* I baptize thee in the name of the Father, and of the Son, and of the Holy Ghost. Amen.

*Then the Priest shall make a cross upon the child's forehead, saying.*

WE receive this child into the congregation of Christ's flock, and do sign him with the sign of the cross, in token that hereafter he shall not be ashamed to confess the faith of Christ crucified, and manfully to fight under his banner against sin, the world, and the devil, and to continue Christ's faithful soldier and servant unto his life's end. Amen.

*Then shall the Priest say.*

SEEING now, dearly beloved brethren, that these children be regenerate and grafted into the body of Christ's congregation: let us give thanks unto God for these benefits, and with one accord make our prayers unto almighty God, that they may lead the rest of their life according to this beginning.

*Then shall be said.*

OUR Father which art in heaven. &c.

*Then shall the Priest say.*

WE yield thee hearty thanks, most merciful Father, that it hath pleased thee to regenerate this infant with thy Holy Spirit, to receive him for thy ⁊ own child by adoption, and to incorporate him into thy holy congregation. And humbly we beseech thee to grant that he, being dead unto sin, and living unto righteousness, and being buried with Christ in his death, may crucify the old man, and utterly abolish the whole body of sin: that as he is made partaker of the death of thy Son, so he may be partaker of his resurrection: so that finally, with the residue of thy holy congregation, he may be inheritor of thine everlasting kingdom: through Christ our Lord. Amen.

*At the last end, the Priest, calling the Godfathers and Godmothers together, shall say this short exhortation following:*

FORASMUCH as these children have promised by you to forsake the devil and all his works, to believe in God, and to serve him; you must remember that it is your parts and duties to see that these infants be taught, so soon as they shall be able to learn, what a solemn vow, promise, and profession they have made by you. And that they may know these things the better, ye shall call upon them to hear sermons:

---

⁊ In some copies, "thine own."

And chiefly ye shall provide that they may learn the Creed, the Lord's Prayer, and the ten Commandments, in the English tongue, and all other things which a Christian man ought to know and believe, to his soul's health: and that these children may be virtuously brought up to lead a godly and Christian life; remembering always that baptism doth represent unto us our profession, which is, to follow the example of our Saviour Christ, and to be made like unto him; that as he died and rose again for us, so should we which are baptized die from sin, and rise again unto righteousness, continually mortifying all our evil and corrupt affections, and daily proceeding in all virtue, and godliness of living.

*The Minister shall command that the children be brought to the Bishop to be confirmed of him, so soon as they can say in their vulgar tongue the articles of the faith, the Lord's prayer, and the x Commandments, and be further instructed in the Catechism, set forth for that purpose, accordingly as it is there expressed.*

## OF THEM THAT BE
## BAPTIZED IN PRIVATE HOUSES,
### IN TIME OF NECESSITY.

*The Pastors and Curates shall oft admonish the people, that they defer not the Baptism of infants any longer than the Sunday, or other holy day next after the child be born, unless upon a great and reasonable cause declared to the Curate and by him approved.*

*And also they shall warn them, that without great cause and necessity, they baptize not children at home in their houses. And when great need shall compel them so to do, that then they minister it on this fashion.*

*First let them that be present call upon God for his grace, and say the Lord's prayer, if the time will suffer. And then one of them shall name the child, and dip him in the water, or pour water upon him, saying these words.*

*N.* I baptize thee in the name of the Father, and of the Son, and of the Holy Ghost. Amen.

*And let them not doubt, but that the child so Baptized, is lawfully and sufficiently Baptized, and ought not to be Baptized again, in the Church. But yet nevertheless, if the child which is after this sort Baptized, do afterward live, it is expedient that he be brought into the church, to the intent the Priest may examine and try, whether the child be lawfully Baptized or no. And if those that bring any child to the church do answer that he is already baptized, then shall the Priest examine them further.*

By whom the child was baptized?
Who was present when the child was baptized?
Whether they called upon God for grace and succour in that necessity?
With what thing, or what matter, they did baptize the child?
With what words the child was baptized?

Whether they think the child to be lawfully and perfectly baptized?

*And if the minister shall prove by the answers of such as brought the child, that all things were done as they ought to be: Then shall not he christen the child again, but shall receive him, as one of the flock of the true Christian people, saying thus.*

I CERTIFY you, that in this case ye have done well, and according unto due order concerning the baptizing of this child, which being born in original sin and in the wrath of God, is now by the laver of regeneration in Baptism received into the number of the children of God, and heirs of everlasting life: for our Lord Jesus Christ doth not deny his grace and mercy unto such infants, but most lovingly doth call them unto him, as the holy Gospel doth witness to our comfort, on this wise.

AT[r] a certain time they brought children unto Christ that he should touch them, and his disciples rebuked those that brought them. But when Jesus saw it, he was displeased, and said unto them: Suffer little children to come unto me, and forbid them not, for to such belongeth the kingdom of God. Verily I say unto you, whosoever doth not receive the kingdom of God as a little child, he shall not enter therein. And when he had taken them up in his arms, he put his hands upon them and blessed them. *Mark x.*

¶ *After the Gospel is read, the Minister shall make this exhortation upon the words of the Gospel.*

FRIENDS, you hear in this Gospel the words of our Saviour Christ, that he commanded the children to be brought unto him: how he blamed those that would have kept them from him: how he exhorted all men to follow their innocency: ye perceive how by his outward gesture and deed he declared his good will

---

[r] In some copies, a heading, "the Gospel," is inserted here.

toward them. For he embraced them in his arms, he laid his hands upon them, and blessed them. Doubt[*] you not therefore, but earnestly believe, that he hath likewise favourably received this present infant, that he hath embraced him with the arms of his mercy, that he hath given unto him the blessing of eternal life, and made him partaker of his everlasting kingdom. Wherefore we being thus persuaded of the good will of our heavenly Father, declared by his Son Jesus Christ towards this infant: Let us faithfully and devoutly give thanks unto him, and say the prayer which the Lord himself taught; and in declaration of our faith, let us recite the articles contained in our Creed.

*Here the Minister with the Godfathers and Godmothers shall say.*

OUR Father which art in heaven, &c.

*Then shall the Priest demand the name of the child, which being by the Godfathers and Godmothers pronounced, the Minister shall say,*

*N.* Dost thou in the name of this child forsake the Devil and all his works, the vain pomp and glory of the world, with all the covetous desires of the same, the carnal desires of the flesh, and not to follow, and be led by them?

*Answer.* I forsake them all.

*Minister.* Dost thou in the name of this child profess this faith, to believe in God the Father almighty, maker of heaven and earth. And in Jesus Christ his only-begotten Son our Lord: and that he was conceived by the Holy Ghost, born of the virgin Mary, that he suffered under Pontius Pilate, was crucified, dead and buried, that he went down into hell, and also did arise again the third day: that he ascended

---

[*] In some copies, " Doubt ye not," and in some copies, " Doubt nót you."

# PRIVATE BAPTISM.

into heaven, and sitteth at the right hand of God the Father almighty: and from thence he shall come again at the end of the world to judge the quick and the dead?

And do you in his name believe in the Holy Ghost. The holy catholic Church. The Communion of saints. The remission of sins. Resurrection, and everlasting life after death?

*Answer.* All this I stedfastly believe.

Let us pray.

ALMIGHTY and everlasting God, heavenly Father, we give thee humble thanks, for that thou hast vouchsafed to call us to the knowledge of thy grace, and faith in thee: increase this knowledge and confirm this faith in us evermore: Give thy Holy Spirit to this infant, that he being born again, and being made heir of everlasting salvation, through our Lord Jesus Christ, may continue thy servant, and attain thy promise, through the same our Lord Jesus Christ thy Son: who liveth and reigneth with thee in unity of the same Holy Spirit everlastingly. Amen.

*Then shall the Minister make this exhortation to the Godfathers, and Godmothers.*

FORASMUCH as this child hath promised by you to forsake the devil and all his works, to believe in God, and to serve him: you must remember that it is your part and duty to see that this infant be taught so soon as he shall be able to learn, what a solemn vow, promise, and profession he hath made by you: and that he may know these things the better, ye shall call upon him to hear sermons: And chiefly ye shall provide that he may learn the Creed, the Lord's prayer, and the ten Commandments in the English tongue, and all other things which a Christian man ought to know and believe, to his soul's health, and that this child may be virtuously brought up, to lead a godly and a Christian life: remembering alway that Baptism doth represent unto us our profession, which is to follow the example of our Saviour Christ, and be made like unto him: that as he died and rose again for us, so should we, which are baptized, die from sin, and rise again unto righteousness, continually mortifying all our evil and corrupt affections, and daily proceeding in all virtue, and godliness of living.

*And so forth, as in Public Baptism.*

*But if they which bring the infants to the church, do make an uncertain answer to the Priest's questions, and say that they cannot tell what they thought, did, or said, in that great fear and trouble of mind (as oftentimes it chanceth): then let the Priest baptize him in form above written concerning Public Baptism, saving that at the dipping of the Child in the Font, he shall use this form of words.*

IF thou be not baptized already, *N.* I baptize thee in the name of the Father, and of the Son, and of the Holy Ghost. Amen.

# CONFIRMATION

## WHEREIN IS CONTAINED A CATECHISM FOR CHILDREN.

*To the end that Confirmation may be ministered to the more edifying of such as shall receive it (according unto Saint Paul's doctrine, who teacheth that all things should be done in the Church to the edification of the same) it is thought good that none hereafter shall be confirmed, but such as can say in their mother tongue the articles of the faith, the Lord's prayer, and the x commandments; And can also answer to such questions of this short Catechism, as the Bishop (or such as he shall appoint) shall by his discretion appose them in. And this order is most convenient to be observed for divers considerations.*

*First, because that when children come to the years of discretion, and have learned what their Godfathers and Godmothers promised for them in Baptism, they may then themselves with their own mouth, and with their own consent, openly before the Church, ratify and confirm the same: and also promise that by the grace of God they will evermore endeavour themselves faithfully to observe and keep such things, as they by their own mouth and confession have assented unto.*

*Secondly, forasmuch as Confirmation is ministered to them that be baptized, that by imposition of hands and prayer they may receive strength and defence against all temptations to sin, and the assaults of the world, and the Devil: it is most meet to be ministered when children come to that age, that partly by the frailty of their own flesh, partly by the assaults of the world and the Devil, they begin to be in danger to fall into sundry kinds of sin.*

*Thirdly, for that it is agreeable with the usage of the Church in times past, whereby it was ordained that Confirmation should be ministered to them that were of perfect age, that they being instructed in Christ's religion, should openly profess their own faith, and promise to be obedient unto the will of God.*

*And that no man shall think that any detriment shall come to children by deferring of their Confirmation: he shall know for truth, that it is certain by God's word, that children being baptized, have all things necessary for their salvation, and be undoubtedly saved.*

# A CATECHISM,

### THAT IS TO SAY,

## AN INSTRUCTION TO BE LEARNED OF EVERY CHILD, BEFORE HE BE BROUGHT TO BE CONFIRMED OF THE BISHOP.

*Question.* WHAT is your name?
*Answer.* N or M.
*Question.* Who gave you this name?
*Answer.* My Godfathers and Godmothers in my baptism, wherein I was made a member of Christ, the child of God, and an inheritor of the kingdom of heaven.
*Question.* What did your Godfathers and Godmothers then for you?
*Answer.* They did promise and vow three things in my name. First, that I should forsake the devil and all his works and pomps, the vanities of the wicked world, and all the sinful lusts of the flesh. Secondly, that I should believe all the articles of the Christian faith. And thirdly, that I should keep God's holy will and commandments, and walk in the same all the days of my life.
*Question.* Dost thou not think that thou art bound to believe and to do as they have promised for thee?
*Answer.* Yes verily. And by God's help so I will. And I heartily thank our heavenly Father, that he hath called me to this state of salvation, through Jesus Christ our Saviour. And I pray God to give me his

grace, that I may continue in the same unto my life's end.

*Question.* Rehearse the articles of thy belief.

*Answer.* I believe in God the Father Almighty, maker of heaven and of earth. And in Jesus Christ his only Son our Lord. Which was conceived of the Holy Ghost, born of the virgin Mary. Suffered under Ponce Pilate, was crucified, dead and buried, he descended into hell. The third day he rose again from the dead. He ascended into heaven, and sitteth at the right hand of God the Father Almighty. From thence he shall come to judge the quick and the dead. I believe in the Holy Ghost. The holy Catholic Church. The communion of saints. The forgiveness of sins. The resurrection of the body. And the life everlasting. Amen.

*Question.* What dost thou chiefly learn in these articles of thy belief?

*Answer.* First, I learn to believe in God the Father, who hath made me and all the world.

Secondly, in God the Son, who hath redeemed me and all mankind.

Thirdly, in God the Holy Ghost, who sanctifieth me and all the elect people of God.

*Question.* You said that your Godfathers and Godmothers did promise for you that you should keep God's commandments. Tell me how many there be.

*Answer.* Ten.

*Question.* Which be they?

*Answer.* The same which God spake in the xx. Chapter of Exodus, saying: I am the Lord thy God which have brought thee out of the land of Egypt, out of the house of bondage.

I. Thou shalt have none other gods but me.

II. Thou shalt not make to thyself any graven image, nor the likeness of any thing that is in heaven above, or in the earth beneath, nor in the water under the earth: thou shalt not bow down to them, nor worship them. For I the Lord thy God am a jealous God, and visit the sins of the fathers upon the children, unto the third and fourth generation of them that hate me, and shew mercy unto thousands in them that love me, and keep my commandments.

III. Thou shalt not take the name of the Lord thy God in vain : for the Lord will not hold him guiltless that taketh his name in vain.

IV. Remember that thou[†] keep holy the Sabbath day. Six days shalt thou labour and do all that thou hast to do : but the seventh day is the Sabbath of the Lord thy God. In it thou shalt do no manner of work, thou, and thy son and thy daughter, thy man servant, and thy maid servant, thy cattle, and the stranger that is within thy gates : for in six days the Lord made heaven and earth, the sea, and all that in them is, and rested the seventh day. Wherefore the Lord blessed the seventh day, and hallowed it.

V. Honour thy father and thy mother, that thy days may be long in the land which the Lord thy God giveth thee.

VI. Thou shalt do no murther.

VII. Thou shalt not commit adultery.

VIII. Thou shalt not steal.

IX. Thou shalt not bear false witness against thy neighbour.

X. Thou shalt not covet thy neighbour's house, thou shalt not covet thy neighbour's wife, nor his servant, nor his maid, nor his ox, nor his ass, nor any thing that is his.

*Question.* What dost thou chiefly learn by these commandments?

*Answer.* I learn two things : My duty towards God, and my duty towards my neighbour.

*Question.* What is thy duty towards God?

*Answer.* My duty towards God is, to believe in him, to fear him, and to love him with all my

---

[†] In some copies, "Remember thou."

heart, with all my mind, with all my soul, and with all my strength. To worship him. To give him thanks. To put my whole trust in him. To call upon him. To honour his holy name and his word, and to serve him truly all the days of my life.

*Question.* What is thy duty towards thy neighbour?

*Answer.* My duty towards my neighbour is, to love him as myself. And to do to all men as I would they should do unto me. To love, honour and succour my father and mother. To honour and obey the King and his ministers. To submit myself to all my governors, teachers, spiritual Pastors, and masters. To order myself lowly and reverently to all my betters. To hurt no body by word nor deed. To be true and just in all my dealing. To bear no malice nor hatred in my heart. To keep my hands from picking and stealing, and my tongue from evil speaking, lying, and slandering. To keep my body in temperance, soberness, and chastity. Not to covet nor desire other men's goods. But learn and labour truly to get mine own living, and to do my duty in that state of life, unto which it shall please God to call me.

*Question.* My good child, know this, that thou art not able to do these things of thyself, nor to walk in the commandments of God, and to serve him, without his special grace, which thou must learn at all times to call for by diligent prayer. Let me hear therefore if thou canst say the Lord's prayer.

*Answer.* Our Father, which art in heaven, hallowed be thy name. Thy kingdom come. Thy will be done in earth as it is in heaven. Give us this day our daily bread. And forgive us our trespasses, as we forgive them that trespass against us. And lead us not into temptation. But deliver us from evil. Amen.

*Question.* What desirest thou of God in this prayer?

*Answer.* I desire my Lord God our heavenly Father, who is the giver of all goodness, to send his grace unto me and to all people, that we may worship him, serve him, and obey him as we ought to do. And I pray unto God, that he will send us all things that be needful both for our souls and bodies: And that he will be merciful unto us, and forgive us our sins: and that it will please him to save and defend us in all dangers ghostly and bodily. And that he will keep us from all sin and wickedness, and from our ghostly enemy, and from everlasting death. And this ᵘ I trust he will do of his mercy and goodness, through our Lord Jesu Christ. And therefore I say, Amen. So be it.

> *So soon as the children can say in their mother tongue the articles of the faith, the Lord's prayer, the x Commandments: and also can answer to such questions of this short Catechism, as the Bishop (or such as he shall appoint) shall by his discretion appose them in: then shall they be brought to the Bishop by one that shall be his Godfather, or Godmother, that every child may have a witness of his Confirmation.*

*And the Bishop shall confirm them on this wise.*

## CONFIRMATION.

Our help is in the name of the Lord.
*Answer.* Which hath made both heaven and earth.
*Minister.* Blessed is the name of the Lord.
*Answer.* Henceforth world without end.
*Minister.* Lord, hear our prayer.
*Answer.* And let our cry come to thee.

Let us pray.
ALMIGHTY and everliving God, who hast vouchsafed to regenerate these thy servants by water and the Holy Ghost, and hast given unto them forgiveness of all their sins: strengthen them, we beseech thee, O Lord, with the Holy Ghost the Comforter, and daily increase in them thy manifold gifts of grace, the spirit of wisdom and understanding; the spirit of

---

ᵘ In some copies, "thus."

counsel and ghostly strength, the spirit of knowledge and true godliness: and fulfil them, O Lord, with the spirit of thy holy fear. Amen.

*Then the Bishop shall lay his hand upon every child severally, saying,*

DEFEND, O Lord, this child with thy heavenly grace, that he may continue thine for ever, and daily increase in thy Holy Spirit more and more, until he come unto thy everlasting kingdom. Amen.

*Then shall the Bishop say.*

Let us pray.

ALMIGHTY everliving God, which makest us both to will, and to do those things that be good and acceptable unto thy Majesty: we make our humble supplications unto thee for these children, upon whom (after the example of thy holy Apostles) we have laid our hands, to certify them (by this sign) of thy favour and gracious goodness toward them: let thy fatherly hand we beseech thee ever be over them, let thy Holy Spirit ever be with them, and so lead them in the knowledge and obedience of thy word, that in the end they may obtain the everlasting life, through our Lord Jesus Christ, who with thee and the Holy Ghost liveth and reigneth one God, world without end. Amen.

*Then the Bishop shall bless the children, thus saying.*

The blessing of God Almighty, the Father, the Son, and the Holy Ghost, be upon you, and remain with you for ever. Amen.

*The Curate of every Parish, or some other at his appointment, shall diligently upon Sundays, and holy days half an hour before evensong\*, openly in the Church instruct and examine so many children of his parish sent unto him,*

\* In some copies, " Evening Prayer."

*as the time will serve, and as he shall think convenient, in some part of this Catechism.*

*And all Fathers, Mothers, Masters, and Dames, shall cause their children, servants, and prentices (which have not learned their Catechism), to come to the church at the time appointed, and obediently to hear and be ordered by the Curate, until such time as they have learned all that is here appointed for them to learn. And whensoever the Bishop shall give knowledge for children to be brought afore him to any convenient place, for their Confirmation: Then shall the Curate of every parish either bring, or send in writing, the names of all those children of his parish which can say the articles of their faith, the Lord's prayer, and the x commandments: and also how many of them can answer to the other questions contained in this Catechism.*

*And there shall none be admitted to the holy Communion, until such time as he can say the Catechism, and be confirmed.*

# THE FORM OF
# SOLEMNIZATION OF MATRIMONY.

*First the banns must be asked three several Sundays or holy days, in the time of service, the people being present after the accustomed manner.*

*And if the persons that would be married dwell in divers Parishes, the banns must be asked in both Parishes, and the Curate of the one Parish shall not solemnize Matrimony betwixt them, without a certificate of the banns being thrice asked, from the Curate of the other Parish. At the day appointed for Solemnization of Matrimony, the persons to be married shall come into the body of the church, with their friends and neighbours. And there the Priest shall thus say.*

DEARLY beloved friends, we are gathered together here in the sight of God, and in the face of his congregation, to join together this man and this woman in holy matrimony, which is an honourable estate, instituted of God in Paradise, in the time of man's innocency, signifying unto us the mystical union that is betwixt Christ and his Church: which holy estate Christ adorned and beautified with his presence, and first miracle that he wrought, in Cana of Galilee, and is commended of Saint Paul to be honourable among all men; and therefore is not to be enterprised, nor taken in hand unadvisedly, lightly, or wantonly, to satisfy men's carnal lusts and appetites, like brute beasts that have no understanding: but reverently, discreetly, advisedly, soberly, and in the fear of God: Duly considering the causes for which Matrimony was ordained. One was the procreation of children, to be brought up in the fear and nurture of the Lord, and praise of God. Secondly it was ordained for a remedy against sin, and to avoid fornication, that such persons as have not the gift of continence, might marry, and keep themselves undefiled members of Christ's body. Thirdly, for the mutual society, help, and comfort, that the one ought to have of the other, both in prosperity and adversity. Into the which holy estate these two persons present come now to be joined. Therefore if any man can shew any just cause, why they may not lawfully be joined together: let him now speak, or else hereafter for ever hold his peace.

*And also speaking to the persons that shall be married, he shall say.*

I require and charge you (as you will answer at the dreadful day of judgment, when the secrets of all hearts shall be disclosed) that if either of you do know any impediment, why ye may not be lawfully joined together in matrimony, that ye confess it. For be ye well assured, that so many as be coupled together otherwise than God's word doth allow, are not joined together by God, neither is their matrimony lawful.

*At which day of marriage if any man do allege and declare any impediment why they may not be coupled together in Matrimony by God's law or the laws of this Realm, and will be bound, and sufficient sureties with him, to the parties, or else put in a caution to the full value of such charges as the persons to be married do[x] sustain, to prove his allegation: then the Solemnization must be deferred, unto such time as the truth be tried. If no impediment be alleged, then shall the Curate say unto the man.*

*N*. Wilt thou have this woman to thy wedded wife, to live together after God's ordinance in the holy estate of Matrimony? Wilt thou love her, comfort her, honour, and keep her in sickness and in health? And forsaking all other keep thee only to her, so long as you both shall live?

[x] In some copies, "doth sustain."

## OF MATRIMONY.

*The man shall answer,*
I will.

*Then shall the Priest say to the woman.*

*N.* Wilt thou have this man to thy wedded husband, to live together after God's ordinance, in the holy estate of Matrimony? Wilt thou obey him, and serve him, love, honour, and keep him, in sickness and in health? and forsaking all other keep thee only unto him, so long as you both shall live?

*The woman shall answer,*
I will.

*Then shall the Minister say,*
Who giveth this woman to be married to this man?

*And the Minister receiving the woman at her father or friend's hands, shall cause the man to take the woman by the right hand, and so either to give their troth to other. The man first saying,*

I *N.* take thee *N.* to my wedded wife, to have and to hold from this day forward, for better, for worse, for richer, for poorer, in sickness, and in health, to love, and to cherish, till death us depart, according to God's holy ordinance: And thereto I plight thee my troth.

*Then shall they loose their hands, and the woman taking again the man by the right hand shall say,*

I *N.* take thee *N.* to my wedded husband, to have and to hold from this day forward, for better, for worse, for richer, for poorer, in sickness, and in health, to love, cherish, and to obey, till death us depart, according to God's holy ordinance: And thereto I give thee my troth.

*Then shall they again loose their hands, and the man shall give unto the woman a ring, laying the same upon the book, with the accustomed duty to the Priest and Clerk. And the Priest taking the ring shall deliver it unto the man, to put it upon the fourth finger of the woman's left hand. And the man taught by the Priest, shall say,*

With this ring I thee wed: with my body I thee worship: and with all my worldly goods I thee endow. In the name of the Father, and of the Son, and of the Holy Ghost. Amen.

*Then the man leaving the ring upon the fourth finger of the woman's left hand, the Minister shall say,*

¶ Let us pray.

O ETERNAL God, creator and preserver of all mankind, giver of all spiritual grace, the author of everlasting life: Send thy blessing upon these thy servants, this man and this woman, whom we bless in thy name, that as Isaac and Rebecca lived faithfully together; so these persons may surely perform and keep the vow and covenant betwixt them made, whereof this ring given and received is a token and pledge: and may ever remain in perfect love and peace together; and live according unto thy laws; through Jesus Christ our Lord. Amen.

¶ *Then shall the Priest join their right hands together, and say,*

Those whom God hath joined together, let no man put asunder.

¶ *Then shall the Minister speak unto the people.*

FORASMUCH as *N*. and *N*. have consented together in holy wedlock, and have witnessed the same before God and this company, and thereto have given and pledged their troth either to other, and have declared the same by giving and receiving of a ring, and by joining of hands: I pronounce that they be man and wife together. In the name of the Father, of the Son, and of the Holy Ghost. Amen.

## OF MATRIMONY.

¶ *And the Minister shall add this blessing.*

God the Father, God the Son, God the Holy Ghost bless, preserve, and keep you: the Lord mercifully with his favour look upon you, and so fill you with all spiritual benediction and grace, that you may so live together in this life, that in the world to come you may have life everlasting. Amen.

¶ *Then the Ministers or Clerks, going to the Lord's table, shall say or sing this Psalm following.*

BLESSED are all they that fear the Lord: and walk in his ways. *Beati omnes. cxxviii.*

For thou shalt eat the labour of thy hands : O well is thee, and happy shalt thou be.

Thy wife shall be as the fruitful vine : upon the walls of thy house.

Thy children like the olive branches : round about thy table.

Lo, thus shall the man be blessed : that feareth the Lord.

The Lord from out of Sion shall bless thee : that thou shalt see Hierusalem in prosperity all thy life long.

Yea, that thou shalt see thy children's children : and peace upon Israel.

Glory be to the Father, &c.

As it was in the, &c.

¶ *Or else this Psalm following.*

GOD be merciful unto us, and bless us : and shew us the light of his countenance, and be merciful unto us. *Deus misereatur. Psalm lxvii.*

That thy way may be known upon the earth : thy saving health among all nations.

Let the people praise thee (O God :) yea, let all the people praise thee.

O let the nations rejoice and be glad : for thou shalt

judge the flock[r] righteously, and govern the nations upon the earth.

Let the people praise thee, O God : let all the people praise thee.

Then shall the earth bring forth her increase : and God, even our own God, shall give us his blessing.

God shall bless us, and all the ends of the world shall fear him.

Glory be to the Father, &c.

As it was in the, &c.

¶ *The Psalm ended, and the man and the woman kneeling afore the Lord's table: the Priest standing at the table, and turning his face toward them, shall say,*

Lord, have mercy upon us.

*Answer.* Christ, have mercy upon us.

*Minister.* Lord, have mercy upon us.

¶ Our Father which art in heaven, &c.

And lead us not into temptation.

*Answer.* But deliver us from evil. Amen.

*Minister.* O Lord, save thy servant, and thy handmaid.

*Answer.* Which put their trust in thee.

*Minister.* O Lord, send them help from thy holy place.

*Answer.* And evermore defend them.

*Minister.* Be unto them a tower of strength.

*Answer.* From the face of their enemy.

*Minister.* O Lord, hear our prayer.

*Answer.* And let our cry come unto thee.

*The Minister.*

O God of Abraham, God of Isaac, God of Jacob, bless these thy servants, and sow the seed of eternal life in their minds, that whatsoever in thy holy word they shall profitably learn, they may in deed fulfil the same. Look, O Lord, mercifully upon them from heaven, and bless them. And as thou didst send

---

[r] In some copies, "folk."

thy blessing upon Abraham and Sara to their great comfort; so vouchsafe to send thy blessing upon these thy servants, that they obeying thy will, and alway being in safety under thy protection, may abide in thy love unto their lives' end: through Jesu Christ our Lord. Amen.

*This prayer next following shall be omitted where the woman is past child-birth*

O MERCIFUL Lord and heavenly Father, by whose gracious gift mankind is increased: we beseech thee, assist with thy blessing these two persons, that they may both be fruitful in procreation of children, and also live together so long in godly love and honesty, that they may see their children's children, unto the third and fourth generation, unto thy praise and honour: through Jesus Christ our Lord. Amen.

O God, which by thy mighty power hast made all things of nought, which also after other things set in order didst appoint that out of man (created after thine own image and similitude) woman should take her beginning: and, knitting them together, didst teach that it should never be lawful to put asunder those, whom thou by matrimony hadst made one: O God, which hast consecrated the state of matrimony to such an excellent mystery, that in it is signified and represented the spiritual marriage and unity betwixt Christ and his church: Look mercifully upon these thy servants, that both this man may love his wife, according to thy word, (as Christ did love his spouse the church, who gave himself for it, loving and cherishing it even as his own flesh;) and also that this woman may be loving and amiable to her husband as Rachel, wise as Rebecca, faithful and obedient as Sara; and in all quietness, sobriety, and peace, be a follower of holy and godly matrons: O Lord, bless them both, and grant them to inherit thy everlasting kingdom: through Jesus Christ our Lord. Amen.

*Then shall the Priest say,*

ALMIGHTY God, which at the beginning did create our first parents Adam and Eve, and did sanctify and join them together in marriage: pour upon you the riches of his grace, sanctify and bless you, that ye may please him both in body and soul, and live together in holy love, unto your lives' end. Amen.

*Then shall begin the Communion, and after the gospel shall be said a sermon, wherein ordinarily (so oft as there is any marriage) the office of a man and wife shall be declared according to holy scripture: or if there be no sermon, the Minister shall read this that followeth.*

ALL ye which be married, or which intend to take the holy estate of matrimony upon you: hear what holy scripture doth say, as touching the duty of husbands toward their wives, and wives toward their husbands. Saint Paul (in his Epistle to the Ephesians the fifth chapter) doth give this commandment to all married men.

Ye husbands, love your wives, even as Christ loved the church, and hath given himself for it, to sanctify it, purging it in the fountain of water, through thy [1] word, that he might make it unto himself a glorious congregation, not having spot, or wrinkle, or any such thing; but that it should be holy and blameless. So men are bound to love their own wives as their own bodies. He that loveth his own wife, loveth himself. For never did any man hate his own flesh, but nourisheth and cherisheth it, even as the Lord doth the congregation; for we are members of his body, of his flesh, and of his bones.

For this cause shall a man leave father and mother, and shall be joined unto his wife, and they two shall be one flesh. This mystery is great, but I speak of Christ and of the congregation. Nevertheless, let every one of you so love his own wife, even as himself.

[1] In some copies, "the word."

Likewise the same Saint Paul (writing to the Colossians) speaketh thus to all men that be married: Ye men, love your wives and be not bitter unto them. Coloss. iii.[a]

Hear also what saint Peter the apostle of Christ, which was himself a married man, saith unto all men that are married. Ye husbands, dwell with your wives according to knowledge: giving honour unto the wife, as unto the weaker vessel, and as heirs together of the grace of life, so that your prayers be not hindered. 1 Pet. iii.

*Hitherto ye have heard the duty of the husband toward the wife.

*Now likewise, ye wives, hear and learn your duty towards your husbands, even as it is plainly set forth in holy scripture.

Saint Paul (in the forenamed Epistle to the Ephesians) teacheth you thus: Ye women submit yourselves unto your own husbands as unto the Lord: for the husband is the wife's head, even as Christ is the head of the Church. And he is also the Saviour of the whole body. Therefore as the church, or congregation, is subject unto Christ: so likewise let the wives also be in subjection unto their own husbands in all things. And again he saith: Let the wife reverence her husband. Ephes. v.

And in his Epistle to the Colossians Saint Paul giveth you this short lesson: Ye wives, submit yourselves unto your own husbands, as it is convenient in the Lord. Coloss. iii.[b]

Saint Peter also doth instruct you very godly, thus saying: Let wives be subject to their own husbands, so that if any obey not the word, they may be won without the word, by the conversation of the wives, while they behold your chaste con- 1 Pet. iii.[c]

---

[a] *Misprinted* Coloss. iv.   * These two paragraphs are in all copies printed in the same type as the rubricks.   [b] *Misprinted* Coloss. ii.   [c] In some copies, *misprinted* 1 Pet. iv.

versation, coupled with fear: whose apparel let it not be outward, with braided hair and trimming about with gold, either in putting on of gorgeous apparel: but let the hid man, which is in the heart, be without all corruption, so that the spirit be mild and quiet, which is a precious thing in the sight of God. For after this manner (in the old time) did the holy women, which trusted in God apparel themselves, being subject to their own husbands: as Sara obeyed Abraham calling him lord, whose daughters ye are made, doing well and being not dismayed with any fear.

*The new married persons (the same day of their marriage) must receive the holy communion.*

# THE ORDER FOR THE VISITATION OF THE SICK.

¶ *The Priest entering into the sick person's house, shall say,*

Peace be in this house, and to all that dwell in it.

*When he cometh into the sick man's presence, he shall say, kneeling down.*

REMEMBER not, Lord, our iniquities, nor the iniquities of our forefathers. Spare us, good Lord, spare thy people, whom thou hast redeemed with thy most precious blood, and be not angry with us for ever.

Lord, have mercy upon us.
Christ, have mercy upon us.
Lord, have mercy upon us.
Our Father, which art in heaven, &c.
And lead us not into temptation.
*Answer.* But deliver us from evil. Amen.
*Minister.* O Lord, save thy servant.
*Answer.* Which putteth his trust in thee.
*Minister.* Send him help from thy holy place.
*Answer.* And evermore mightily defend him.
*Minister.* Let the enemy have none advantage of him.
*Answer.* Nor the wicked approach to hurt him.
*Minister.* Be unto him, O Lord, a strong tower.
*Answer.* From the face of his enemy.
*Minister.* Lord, hear our prayers.
*Answer.* And let our cry come unto thee.

*Minister.*

O LORD, look down from heaven, behold, visit, and relieve this thy servant: Look upon him with the eyes of thy mercy, give him comfort, and sure confidence in thee: Defend him from the danger of the enemy, and keep him in perpetual peace, and safety: through Jesus Christ our Lord. Amen.

Hear us, Almighty and most merciful God and Saviour. Extend thy accustomed goodness to this thy servant, which is grieved with sickness: Visit him, O Lord, as thou didst visit Peter's wife's mother and the Captain's servant. So visit and restore unto this sick person his former health, (if it be thy will,) or else give him grace so to take thy visitation, that after this painful life ended, he may dwell with thee in life everlasting. Amen.

*Then shall the Minister exhort the sick person after this form or other like.*

DEARLY beloved, know this: that Almighty God is the Lord of life and death, and over all things to them pertaining, as youth, strength, health, age, weakness, and sickness. Wherefore, whatsoever your sickness is, know you certainly, that it is God's visitation. And for what cause soever this sickness is sent unto you: whether it be to try your patience for the example of other, and that your faith may be found in the day of the Lord laudable, glorious, and honourable, to the increase of glory, and endless felicity: or else it be sent unto you to correct and amend in you, whatsoever doth offend the eyes of our heavenly Father: know you certainly, that if you truly repent you of your sins, and bear your sickness patiently, trusting in God's mercy, for his dear Son Jesus Christ's sake, and render unto him humble thanks for his fatherly visitation, submitting yourself wholly to his will; it shall turn to your profit, and help you forward in the right way that leadeth unto everlasting life.

¶ *If the person visited be very sick, then the Curate may end his exhortation at this place.*

¶ Take therefore in good worth the chastement of the Lord: For whom the Lord loveth, he chastiseth.

Yea, (as Saint Paul saith,) he scourgeth every son which he receiveth: if you endure chastisement, he offereth himself unto you as unto his own children. What son is he that the father chastiseth not? If ye be not under correction (whereof all true children are partakers), then are ye bastards and not children. Therefore seeing that when our carnal fathers do correct us, we reverently obey them: shall we not now much rather be obedient to our spiritual Father, and so live? And they for a few days do chastise us after their own pleasure: but he doth chastise us for our profit, to the intent he may make us partakers of his holiness. These words, good brother, are God's words, and written in holy scripture for our comfort and instruction, that we should patiently and with thanksgiving bear our heavenly Father's correction, whensoever by any manner of adversity it shall please his gracious goodness to visit us. And there should be no greater comfort to christian persons, than to be made like unto Christ, by suffering patiently adversities, troubles, and sicknesses. For he himself went not up to joy, but first he suffered pain: he entered not into his glory, before he was crucified. So truly our way to eternal joy is to suffer here with Christ, and our door to enter into eternal life is gladly to die with Christ, that we may rise again from death, and dwell with him in everlasting life. Now therefore taking your sickness, which is thus profitable for you, patiently: I exhort you in the name of God, to remember the profession which you made unto God in your Baptism. And forasmuch as after this life there is account to be given unto the righteous Judge, of whom all must be judged without respect of persons: I require you to examine yourself, and your state, both toward God and man: so that accusing and condemning yourself for your own faults, you may find mercy at our heavenly Father's hand for Christ's sake, and not be accused and condemned in that fearful judgment. Therefore I shall shortly rehearse the articles of our faith, that ye may know whether you do believe as a christian man should, or no.

*Here the Minister shall rehearse the articles of the faith, saying thus.*

DOST thou believe in God the Father Almighty?

¶ *And so forth, as it is in Baptism.*

¶ *Then shall the Minister examine whether he be in charity with all the world: Exhorting him to forgive from the bottom of his heart all persons that have offended him: and if he have offended other to ask them forgiveness: And where he hath done injury or wrong to any man, that he make amends to the uttermost of his power. And if he have not afore disposed his goods, let him then make his will. But men must be oft admonished that they set an order for their temporal goods and lands when they be in health. And also declare his debts, what he oweth, and what is owing unto him, for discharging of his conscience, and quietness of his executors.*

¶ *These words before rehearsed, may be said before the Minister begin his prayer, as he shall see cause.*

*The Minister may not forget nor omit to move the sick person (and that most earnestly) to liberality toward the poor.*

¶ *Here shall the sick person make a special confession, if he feel his conscience troubled with any weighty matter. After which confession the Priest shall absolve him after this sort.*

OUR Lord Jesus Christ, who hath left power to his Church to absolve all sinners, which truly repent and believe in him, of his great mercy forgive thee[d] thine offences: and by his authority committed to me, I absolve thee from all thy sins, in the name of the Father, and of the Son, &c. Amen.

[d] In some copies, "thee" *omitted.*

# THE VISITATION OF THE SICK.

¶ *And then the Priest shall say the Collect following.*

¶ Let us pray.

O MOST merciful God, which according to the multitude of thy mercies dost so put away the sins of those which truly repent, that thou rememberest them no more: open thy eye of mercy upon this thy servant, who most earnestly desireth pardon and forgiveness: Renew in him, most loving Father, whatsoever hath been decayed by the fraud and malice of the devil, or by his own carnal will, and frailness: preserve and continue this sick member in the unity of thy church, consider his contrition, accept his tears, assuage his pain, as shall be seen to thee most expedient for him. And forasmuch as he putteth his full trust only in thy mercy; impute not unto him his former sins, but take him unto\* thy favour: through the merits of thy most dearly beloved Son Jesus Christ. Amen.

*Then the Minister shall say this Psalm.*

IN thee, O Lord, have I put my trust, let me never be put to confusion: but rid me, and deliver me, into thy righteousness; incline thine ear unto me, and save me. *In te Domine speravi.* Psal. 71. ᶠ

Be thou my strong hold, (whereunto I may alway resort) thou hast promised to help me, for thou art my house of defence, and my castle.

Deliver me (O my God) out of the hand of the ungodly: out of the hand of the unrighteous and cruel man.

For thou (O Lord God) art the thing that I long for: thou art my hope, even from my youth.

Through thee have I been holden up ever since I was born, thou art he that took me out of my mother's womb; my praise shall be always of thee.

\* In some copies, "to."      ᶠ *Misprinted* Psalm xxi.

I am become as it were a monster unto many : but my sure trust is in thee.

O let my mouth be filled with thy praise (that I may sing of thy glory) and honour all the day long.

Cast me not away in the time of age, forsake me not when my strength faileth me.

For mine enemies speak against me : and they that lay wait for my soul take their counsel together, saying : God hath forsaken him ; persecute him, and take him, for there is none to deliver him.

Go not far from me, O God : my God, haste thee to help me.

Let them be confounded and perish that are against my soul : let them be covered with shame and dishonour that seek to do me evil.

As for me, I will patiently abide alway : and will praise thee more and more.

My mouth shall daily speak of thy righteousness and salvation : for I know no end thereof.

I will go forth in the strength of the Lord God : and will make mention of thy righteousness only.

Thou (O God) hast taught me from my youth up until now : therefore will I tell of thy wondrous works.

Forsake me not (O God) in mine old age, when I am gray-headed, until I have shewed thy strength unto this generation, and thy power to all them that are yet for to come.

Thy righteousness (O God) is very high : and great things are they that thou hast done ; O God, who is like unto thee ?

O what great troubles and adversities hast thou shewed me ! and yet didst thou turn and refresh me : yea, and broughtest me from the deep of the earth again.

Thou hast brought me to great honour : and comforted me on every side.

Therefore will I praise thee and thy faithfulness (O God) playing upon an instrument of musick, unto thee will I sing upon the harp, O thou holy one of Israel.

My lips will be fain when I sing unto thee : and so will my soul whom thou hast delivered.

My tongue also shall talk of thy righteousness all the day long, for they are confounded and brought unto shame that seek to do me evil.

Glory to the Father, &c.

As it was in the beginning, &c.

¶ *Adding this.*

O SAVIOUR of the world, save us, which by thy cross and precious blood hast redeemed us, help us, we beseech thee, O God.

*Then shall the Minister say,*

THE Almighty Lord, which is a most strong tower to all them that put their trust in him, to whom all things in heaven, in earth, and under earth, do bow and obey: be now and evermore thy defence, and make thee know and feel, that there is no other name under heaven given to man, in whom, and through whom, thou mayest receive health and salvation, but only the name of our Lord Jesus Christ. Amen.

# THE COMMUNION OF THE SICK.

*Forasmuch as all mortal men be subject to many sudden perils, diseases and sicknesses, and ever uncertain what time they shall depart out of this life: Therefore to the intent they may be always in a readiness to die, whensoever it shall please Almighty God to call them, the Curates shall diligently from time to time, but specially in the plague time, exhort their parishioners to the oft receiving (in the church) of the holy Communion of the body and blood of our Saviour Christ: which if they do, they shall have no cause, in their sudden visitation, to be unquieted for lack of the same. But if the sick person be not able to come to the church, and yet is desirous to receive the communion in his house, then he must give knowledge over night, or else early in the morning to the Curate, signifying also how many be appointed to communicate with him. And having a convenient place in the sick man's house, where the Curate may reverently minister, and a good number to receive the communion with the sick person, with all things necessary for the same, he shall there minister the holy communion.*

### The Collect.

ALMIGHTY everliving God, Maker of mankind, which dost correct those whom thou dost love, and chastisest every one whom thou dost receive: we beseech thee to have mercy upon this thy servant visited with thy hand, and to grant that he may take his sickness patiently, and recover his bodily health (if it be thy gracious will), and whensoever his soul shall depart from the body, it may be without spot presented unto thee: through Jesus Christ our Lord. Amen [g].

### The Epistle.

MY son, despise not the correction of the Lord, neither faint when thou art rebuked of him: For whom the Lord loveth, him he correcteth, yea and he scourgeth every son, whom he receiveth. Heb. xii.

[g] In some copies, "Amen" omitted.

*The Gospel.*

VERILY, verily I say unto you, he that heareth my word, and believeth on him that sent me, hath everlasting life, and shall not come unto damnation, but he passeth from death unto life.  John v.

¶ *At the time of the distribution of the holy Sacrament, the Priest shall first receive the communion himself, and after minister unto them that be appointed to communicate with the sick.*

¶ *But if any man either by reason of extremity of sickness, or for lack of warning in due time to the Curate, or for lack of company to receive with him, or by any other just impediment, do not receive the Sacrament of Christ's body and blood; then the curate shall instruct him, that if he do truly repent him of his sins, and stedfastly believe that Jesus Christ hath suffered death upon the cross for him, and shed his blood for his redemption, earnestly remembering the benefits he hath thereby, and giving him hearty thanks therefore; he doth eat and drink the body and blood of our Saviour Christ, profitably to his soul's health, although he do not receive the Sacrament with his mouth.*

¶ *When the sick person is visited and receiveth the holy communion all at one time: then the priest for more expedition shall cut off the form of the visitation at the Psalm,* In thee, O Lord, have I put my trust, *and go straight to the communion.*

¶ *In the time of plague, sweat, or such other like contagious times of sicknesses or diseases, when none of the parish or neighbours can be gotten to communicate with the sick in their houses, for fear of the infection, upon special request of the diseased, the minister may alonely communicate with him.*

# THE ORDER FOR THE BURIAL OF THE DEAD.

*The Priest meeting the corpse at the Church stile, shall say: Or else the priests and clerks shall sing, and so go either unto the church, or towards the grave.*

I AM the resurrection and the life saith the Lord: he that believeth in me, yea, though he were dead, yet shall he live. And whosoever liveth and believeth in me, shall not die for ever.   John xi.

I KNOW that my Redeemer liveth, and that I shall rise out of the earth in the last day, and shall be covered again with my skin, and shall see God in my flesh : yea, and I myself shall behold him, not with other but with these same eyes.   Job xix.

WE brought nothing into this world, neither may we carry any thing out of this world. The Lord giveth, and the Lord taketh away. Even as it hath pleased the Lord, so cometh things to pass : blessed be the name of the Lord.   1 Tim. vi. Job i.

*When they come at*[h] *the grave, whiles the corpse is made ready to be laid into the earth, the Priest shall say, or else the Priest and clerks shall sing.*

MAN that is born of a woman, hath but a short time to live, and is full of misery : he cometh up and is cut down like a flower; he flieth as it were a shadow, and never continueth in one stay.   Job xiv.[1]

In the midst of life we be in death : of whom may we seek for succour, but of thee, O Lord, which for our sins justly art displeased? Yet, O Lord God

---

[h] In some copies, "to the grave."   [1] In some copies, *mispr.* Job ix.

most holy, O Lord most mighty, O holy and most merciful Saviour, deliver us not into the bitter pains of eternal death. Thou knowest, Lord, the secrets of our hearts : shut not up thy merciful eyes to our prayers : But spare us, Lord most holy, O God most mighty, O holy and merciful Saviour, thou most worthy Judge eternal, suffer us not at our last hour for any pains of death to fall from thee.

*Then while the earth shall be cast upon the body, by some standing by, the Priest shall say,*

FORASMUCH as it hath pleased almighty God of his great mercy to take unto himself the soul of our dear brother here departed : we therefore commit his body to the ground, earth to earth, ashes to ashes, dust to dust, in sure and certain hope of resurrection to eternal life, through our Lord Jesus Christ, who shall change our vile body, that it may be like to his glorious body, according to the mighty working whereby he is able to subdue all things to himself.

¶ *Then shall be said or sung,*

I HEARD a voice from heaven, saying unto me : Write : from henceforth blessed are the dead which die in the Lord. Even so saith the Spirit, that they rest from their labours.

*Then shall follow this lesson, taken out of the fifteenth Chapter to the Corinthians, the first Epistle.*

CHRIST is risen from the dead, and become the firstfruits of them that slept. For by a man came death, and by a man came the resurrection of the dead. For as by Adam all die, even so by Christ shall all be made alive, but every man in his own order. The first is Christ, then they that are Christ's, at his coming. Then cometh the end, when he hath delivered up the kingdom to God the Father, when he hath put down all rule and all authority and power. For he must reign till he have put all his

1 Cor. 15.

enemies under his feet. The last enemy that shall be destroyed is death. For he hath put all things under his feet. But when he saith all things are put under him, it is manifest that he is excepted, which did put all things under him. When all things are subdued unto him, then shall the Son also himself be subject unto him that put all things under him, that God may be all in all. Else what do they which are baptized over the dead, if the dead rise not at all? Why are they then baptized over them? yea and why stand we alway then in jeopardy? By our rejoicing, which I have in Christ Jesu our Lord, I die daily. That I have fought with beasts at Ephesus after the manner of men, what advantageth it me, if the dead rise not again? Let us eat, and drink, for to-morrow we shall die. Be not ye deceived: evil words corrupt good manners. Awake truly out of sleep, and sin not. For some have not the knowledge of God. I speak this to your shame. But some man will say: How arise the dead? with what body shall they come? Thou fool, that which thou sowest is not quickened, except it die. And what sowest thou? Thou sowest not that body that shall be; but bare corn as of wheat, or of some other: but God giveth it a body at his pleasure, to every seed his own body. All flesh is not one manner of flesh : but there is one manner of flesh of men, another manner of flesh of beasts, another of fishes, another of birds. There are also celestial bodies, and there are bodies terrestrial. But the glory of the celestial is one, and the glory of the terrestrial is another. There is one manner glory of the sun, and another glory of the moon, and another glory of the stars. For one star differeth from another in glory. So is the resurrection of the dead. It is sown in corruption, it riseth again in incorruption. It is sown in dishonour, it riseth again in honour. It is sown in weakness, it riseth again in power. It is sown a natural body, it riseth again a spiritual body. There is a natural body, and there is a spiritual body: as it is also written: The first man Adam was made a living soul, and the last Adam was made a quickening Spirit. Howbeit, that is not first which is spiritual: but that which is natural, and then that which is spiritual. The first man is of the earth, earthy: the second man is the Lord from heaven (heavenly). As is the earthy, such are they that are earthy. And as is the heavenly, such are they that are heavenly. And as we have borne the image of the earthy, so shall we bear the image of the heavenly. This say I, brethren, that flesh and blood cannot inherit the kingdom of God: neither doth corruption inherit uncorruption. Behold, I shew you a mystery. We shall not all sleep: but we shall all be changed and that in a moment, in the twinkling of an eye by the last trump. For the trump shall blow, and the dead shall rise incorruptible, and we shall be changed. For this corruptible must put on incorruption: and this mortal must put on immortality. When this corruptible hath put on incorruption, and this mortal hath put on immortality: then shall be brought to pass the saying that is written: Death is swallowed up in victory: Death, where is thy sting? Hell, where is thy victory? The sting of death is sin: and the strength of sin is the law. But thanks be unto God which hath given us victory, through our Lord Jesus Christ. Therefore, my dear brethren, be ye stedfast, and unmoveable, always rich in the work of the Lord, forasmuch as ye know that your labour is not in vain in the Lord.

*The lesson ended, then the Priest shall say,*

Lord, have mercy upon us.
Christ, have mercy upon us.
Lord, have mercy upon us.
¶ Our Father which art in heaven, &c.
And lead us not into temptation.
*Answer.* But deliver us from evil. Amen.

*The Priest.*

ALMIGHTY God, with whom do live the spirits of them that depart hence in the Lord, and in whom the souls of them that be elected, after they be delivered from the burden of the flesh, be in joy and felicity: We give thee hearty thanks, for that it hath pleased thee to deliver this *N.* our brother out of the miseries of this sinful world: beseeching thee, that it may please thee of thy gracious goodness, shortly to accomplish the number of thine elect, and to haste thy kingdom, that we with this our brother, and all other departed in the true faith of thy holy name, may have our perfect consummation and bliss, both in body and soul, in thy eternal and everlasting glory. Amen.

*The Collect.*

O MERCIFUL God, the Father of our Lord Jesus Christ, who is the resurrection and the life, in whom whosoever believeth, shall live though he die; and whosoever liveth and believeth in him, shall not die eternally: who also taught us (by his holy apostle Paul) not to be sorry, as men without hope, for them that sleep in him: We meekly beseech thee (O Father) to raise us from the death of sin unto the life of righteousness, that when we shall depart this life, we may rest in him, as our hope is this our brother doth; and that at the general resurrection in the last day, we may be found acceptable in thy sight, and receive that blessing which thy wellbeloved Son shall then pronounce to all that love and fear thee, saying: Come, ye blessed children of my Father, receive the kingdom prepared for you from the beginning of the world. Grant this we beseech thee, O merciful Father, through Jesus Christ our Mediator and Redeemer. Amen.

# THE THANKSGIVING OF WOMEN AFTER CHILD BIRTH,

## COMMONLY CALLED

# THE CHURCHING OF WOMEN.

*The woman shall come into the church, and there shall kneel down in some convenient place, nigh unto the place where the table standeth: and the Priest standing by her, shall say these words, or such like, as the case shall require.*

FORASMUCH as it hath pleased Almighty God of his goodness to give you safe deliverance, and hath preserved you in the great danger of child birth: ye shall therefore give hearty thanks unto God, and pray.

*Then shall the Priest say this Psalm.*

I HAVE lifted up mine eyes unto the hills: from whence cometh my help? *Levavi oculos.*
My help cometh even from the Lord: Psalm cxxi. which hath made heaven and earth.

He will not suffer thy foot to be moved: and he that keepeth thee will not sleep.

Behold, he that keepeth Israel: shall neither slumber nor sleep.

The Lord himself is thy keeper: the Lord is thy defence upon thy right hand.

So that the Sun shall not burn thee by day: neither the Moon by night.

The Lord shall preserve thee from all evil: yea, it is even he that shall keep thy soul.

The Lord shall preserve thy going out, and thy coming in: from this time forth for evermore.

Glory be to the Father, and to the Son, and to, &c.

As it was in the beginning, is now and, &c.

 Lord, have mercy upon us.
 Christ, have mercy upon us.
 Lord, have mercy upon us.

¶ Our Father, which, &c.
And lead us not into temptation.
*Answer.* But deliver us from evil. Amen.
*Priest.* O Lord, save this woman thy servant.
*Answer.* Which putteth her trust in thee.
*Priest.* Be thou to her a strong tower.
*Answer.* From the face of her enemy.
*Priest.* Lord, hear our prayer.
*Answer.* And let our cry come unto thee.

*Priest.* ¶ Let us pray.

O ALMIGHTY God, which hast delivered this woman thy servant from the great pain and peril of child birth: Grant, we beseech thee, most merciful Father, that she through thy help may both faithfully live, and walk in her vocation, according to thy will in this life present; and also may be partaker of everlasting glory in the life to come: through Jesus Christ our Lord. Amen.

*The woman that cometh to give her thanks, must offer accustomed offerings: and if there be a Communion, it is convenient that she receive the holy Communion.*

# A COMMINATION AGAINST SINNERS,

## WITH CERTAIN PRAYERS TO BE USED DIVERS TIMES IN THE YEAR.

¶ *After Morning prayer, the people being called together by the ringing of a bell, and assembled in the Church, the English Litany shall be said after the accustomed manner: which ended, the Priest shall go into the pulpit and say thus:*

BRETHREN, in the primitive church there was a Godly discipline, that at the beginning of Lent such persons as were notorious sinners, were put to open penance and punished in this world, that their souls might be saved in the day of the Lord; and that others[j] admonished by their example, might be more afraid to offend. In the stead whereof, until the said discipline may be restored again, which thing is much to be wished, it is thought good, that at this time (in your presence) should be read the general sentences of God's cursing against impenitent sinners, gathered out of the xxvii. Chapter of Deuteronomy, and other places of scripture: and that ye should answer to every sentence, Amen. To the intent that you, being admonished of the great indignation of God against sinners, may the rather be called to earnest and true repentance, and may walk more warily in these dangerous days, fleeing[k] from such vices, for the which ye affirm with your own mouths the curse of God to be due.

CURSED is the man that maketh any carved or molten Image, an abomination to the Lord, the work of the hands of the craftsman, and putteth it in a secret place to worship it.

*And the people shall answer and say,*
Amen.

---

[j] In some copies, "other."   [k] In some copies, "flying."

*Minister.* Cursed is he that curseth his father, and mother.
*Answer.* Amen.
*Minister.* Cursed is he that removeth away the mark of his neighbour's land.
*Answer.* Amen.
*Minister.* Cursed is he that maketh the blind to go out of his way.
*Answer.* Amen.
*Minister.* Cursed is he that letteth in judgment the right of the stranger, of them that be fatherless, and of widows.
*Answer.* Amen.
*Minister.* Cursed is he that smiteth his neighbour secretly.
*Answer.* Amen.
*Minister.* Cursed is he that lieth with his neighbour's wife.
*Answer.* Amen.
*Minister.* Cursed is he that taketh reward to slay the soul of innocent blood.
*Answer.* Amen.
*Minister.* Cursed is he that putteth his trust in man, and taketh man for his defence, and in his heart goeth from the Lord.
*Answer.* Amen.
*Minister.* Cursed are the unmerciful, the fornicators and adulterers, the covetous persons, the worshippers of images, slanderers, drunkards, and extortioners.
*Answer.* Amen.
*The Minister.* Now seeing that all they be accursed (as the prophet David beareth witness) which do err and go astray from the com- Psal. cxviii.[1] mandments of God : let us (remembering the dreadful judgment hanging over our heads, and being always at hand) return unto our Lord God, with all contrition and meekness of heart, bewailing and lament-

[1] In some copies, *mispr.* Ps. cxvii.

ing our sinful life, knowledging and confessing our offences, and seeking to bring forth worthy fruits of penance. For now is the axe put unto the root of the trees, so that every tree which bringeth not forth good fruit, is hewn down, and cast into the fire. It is a fearful thing to fall into the hands of the living God: he shall pour down rain upon the sinners, snares, fire and brimstone, storm and tempest: this shall be their portion to drink. For lo, the Lord is coming out of his place, to visit the wickedness of such as dwell upon the earth. But who may abide the day of his coming? Who shall be able to endure when he appeareth? His fan is in his hand, and he will purge his floor, and gather his wheat into the barn: but he will burn the chaff with unquenchable fire. The day of the Lord cometh as a thief upon the night; and when men shall say peace, and all things are safe, then shall suddenly destruction come upon them, as sorrow cometh upon a woman travailing with child, and they shall not escape: then shall appear the wrath of God in the day of vengeance, which obstinate sinners, through the stubbornness of their heart, have heaped unto themself, which despised the goodness, patience, and long-sufferance of God, when he called them continually to repentance. Then shall they call upon me, saith the Lord, but I will not hear: they shall seek me early, but they shall not find me, and that because they hated knowledge, and received not the fear of the Lord, but abhorred my counsel, and despised my correction: then shall it be too late to knock, when the door shall be shut, and too late to cry for mercy, when it is the time of justice. O terrible voice of

*Mat. iii.*
*Hebr. x.*
*Psalm x.*
*Esai. xxvi.*
*Mal. iii.*ᵐ
*Mat. iii.*
*1 Thess. v.*ᵃ
*Rom. ii.*
*Prov. i.*

---

ᵐ In some copies, *mispr.* Mal. xxv.   ᵃ In some copies, reference omitted.

most just judgment, which shall be pronounced upon them, when it shall be said unto them: Go ye cursed into the fire everlasting, which is prepared for the devil and his Angels. Math. xxv. Therefore, brethren, take we heed betime [o], while the day of salvation lasteth, for the night cometh when none can work: but let us, 2 Cor. vi. John ix. while we have the light, believe in the light, and walk as the children of the light, that we be not cast into the utter darkness, where is weeping and gnashing of teeth. Mat. xxv. Let us not abuse the goodness of God, which calleth us mercifully to amendment, and of his endless pity promiseth us forgiveness of that which is past, if (with a whole mind and a true heart) we return unto him: for though our sins be red [p] as scarlet, they shall be as white as snow; and [q] though they be like Esai. i. Ezechiel xviii.[r] purple, yet shall they be as white as wool. Turn you clean (saith the Lord) from all your wickedness, and your sin shall not be your destruction. Cast away from you all your ungodliness that ye have done, make you new hearts, and a new spirit: wherefore will ye die, O ye house of Israel? Seeing that I have no pleasure in the death of him that dieth? saith the Lord God. Turn you then, and you shall live. Although we have sinned, yet have we an Advocate with the Father, Jesus Christ the righteous: and he 1 John ii. it is that obtaineth grace for our sins; for he was wounded for our offences, and smitten for our wickedness. Esai. liii. Let us therefore return unto him, who is the merciful receiver of all true penitent sinners, assuring ourself, that he is ready to receive us, and most willing to pardon us, if we come to him with faithful repentance: if we will submit ourselves unto him, and from henceforth walk in his ways: if we will take his easy yoke Math. xi.

[o] In some copies, "by time."    [p] In some copies, "as red as."
[q] In some copies, "and" *omitted*.    [r] In some copies, *mispr.* Ezech. xvii.; others, xxviii.

and light burden upon us, to follow him in lowliness, patience, and charity, and be ordered by the governance of his Holy Spirit, seeking always his glory, and serving him duly in our vocation, with thanksgiving. This if we do, Christ will deliver us from the curse of the law, and from the extreme malediction, which shall light upon them that shall be set on the left hand: and he will set us on his right hand, and give us the blessed benediction of his Father, commanding us to take possession of his glorious kingdom; unto the which he vouchsafe to bring us all, for his infinite mercy. Amen. *Math. xxv.*

*Then shall they all kneel upon their knees: and the Priests and clerks kneeling (where they are accustomed to say the Litany) shall say this Psalm.*

HAVE mercy upon me, (O God,) after thy great goodness: according to the multitude of thy mercies, do away mine offences. *Miserere mei Deus. Psal. li.*

Wash me throughly from my wickedness, and cleanse me from my sin.

For I knowledge my faults, and my sin is ever before me.

Against thee only have I sinned, and done this evil in thy sight : that thou mightest be justified in thy saying, and clear when thou art judged.

Behold, I was shapen in wickedness, and in sin hath my mother conceived me.

But lo, thou requirest truth in the inward parts, and shalt make me to understand wisdom secretly.

Thou shalt purge me with hyssop, and I shall be clean : thou shalt wash me, and I shall be whiter than snow.

Thou shalt make me hear of joy and gladness, that the bones which thou hast broken may rejoice.

Turn thy face from my sins, and put out all my misdeeds.

Make me a clean heart, (O God) and renew a right spirit within me.

Cast me not away from thy presence, and take not thy holy Spirit from me.

O give me the comfort of thy help again, and stablish me with thy free spirit.

Then shall I teach thy ways unto the wicked, and sinners shall be converted unto thee.

Deliver me from blood-guiltiness, (O God,) thou that art the God of my health: and my tongue shall sing of thy righteousness.

Thou shalt open my lips, (O Lord) and my mouth shall shew thy praise.

For thou desirest no sacrifice, else would I give it thee: but thou delightest not in burnt-offering.

The sacrifice of God is a troubled spirit, a broken and contrite heart, (O God,) shalt thou not despise.

O be favourable and gracious unto Sion, build thou the walls of Jerusalem.

Then shalt thou be pleased with the sacrifice of righteousness, with the burnt-offerings and oblations: then shall they offer young bullocks upon thine altar.

Glory be to the Father, &c.
As it was in the beginning, &c.

> Lord, have mercy upon us.
> Christ, have mercy upon us.
> Lord, have mercy upon us.

¶ Our Father, which art in heaven, &c.
And lead us not into temptation.

*Answer.* But deliver us from evil. Amen.
*Minister.* O Lord save thy servants.
*Answer.* Which put their trust in thee.
*Minister.* Send unto them help from above.
*Answer.* And evermore mightily defend them.
*Minister.* Help us, O God our Saviour.
*Answer.* And for the glory of thy name's sake de-

liver us, be merciful unto us sinners for thy name's sake.

*Minister.* O Lord, hear our prayers.

*Answer.* And let our cry come to thee.

Let us pray.

O LORD, we beseech thee mercifully hear our prayers, and spare all those which confess their sins to thee, that they (whose consciences by sin are accused,) by thy merciful pardon may be absolved: Through Christ our Lord. Amen.

O MOST mighty God and merciful Father, which hast compassion of all men, and hatest nothing that thou hast made: which wouldest not the death of a sinner, but that he should rather turn from sin, and be saved: mercifully forgive us our trespasses, receive and comfort us, which be grieved and wearied with the burden of our sin. Thy property is to have mercy; to thee only it appertaineth to forgive sins: spare us therefore, good Lord, spare thy people whom thou hast redeemed. Enter not into judgment with thy servants, which be vile earth, and miserable sinners: but so turn thy* ire from us, which meekly knowledge our vileness, and truly repent us of our faults: so make haste to help us in this world, that we may ever live with thee, in the world to come: through Jesus Christ our Lord. Amen.

¶ *Then shall the people say this that followeth, after the Minister.*

TURN thou us, good Lord, and so shall we be turned: be favourable (O Lord) be favourable to thy people, which turn to thee in weeping, fasting and praying: for thou art a merciful God, full of compassion, long suffering, and of a great pity: Thou

---

* In some copies, "thine ire."

sparest when we deserve punishment, and in thy wrath thinkest upon mercy. Spare thy people, good Lord, spare them, and let not thine ᵗ heritage be brought to confusion: Hear us (O Lord) for thy mercy is great, and after the multitude of thy mercies look upon us.

ᵗ In some copies, "thy heritage."

[THE PSALTER does not appear foliated as part of the book in any of the editions, but is printed so that it can be bound up with them.]

# The fourme

### and maner of makynge and consecratyng Bishoppes, Priestes, and Deacons.

*Anno Domini.* M.D.L.II.[a]

## THE PREFACE.

IT is evident unto all men, diligently reading holy Scripture, and ancient authors, that from the Apostles' time there hath been these orders of Ministers in Christ's church: Bishops, Priests, and Deacons: which Offices were evermore had in such reverent estimation, that no man by his own private authority might presume to execute any of them, except he were first called, tried, examined, and known to have such qualities as were requisite for the same; and also, by public prayer, with imposition of hands, approved, and admitted thereunto. And therefore, to the intent these orders should be continued, and reverently used, and esteemed, in this Church of England, it is requisite, that no man (not being at this present Bishop, Priest, nor Deacon) shall execute any of them, except he be called, tried, examined, and admitted, according to the form hereafter following. And none shall be admitted a Deacon, except he be

---

[a] In one edition, "*Anno a salutifero Virginis partu,*" 1552.

xxi years of age at the least. And every man which is to be admitted a Priest, shall be full xxiv years old. And every man, which is to be consecrated a Bishop, shall be fully thirty years of age. And the Bishop knowing, either by himself, or by sufficient testimony, any person to be a man of virtuous conversation, and without crime, and after examination and trial, finding him learned in the Latin tongue, and sufficiently instructed in holy Scripture, may, upon a Sunday or holy day, in the face of the church, admit him a Deacon, in such manner and form, as hereafter followeth.

# THE FORM AND MANNER OF ORDERING OF DEACONS.

*First, when the day appointed by the Bishop is come, there shall be an exhortation, declaring the duty and office of such as come to be admitted Ministers, how necessary such orders are in the church of Christ, and also, how the people ought to esteem them in their vocation.*

¶ *After the Exhortation ended, the Archdeacon, or his deputy, shall present such as come to the Bishop to be admitted, saying these words.*

REVEREND Father in GOD, I present unto you these persons present, to be admitted Deacons.

¶ *The Bishop.* Take heed that the persons whom ye present unto us, be apt and meet, for their learning, and godly conversation, to exercise their ministry duly, to the honour of GOD, and edifying of his Church.

*The Archdeacon shall answer.*

I have enquired of them, and also examined them, and think them so to be.

¶ *And then the Bishop shall say unto the people,*

BRETHREN, if there be any of you, who knoweth any impediment, or notable crime, in any of these persons presented to be ordered Deacons, for the which he ought not to be admitted to the same, let him come forth, in the name of GOD, and shew what the crime, or impediment is.

¶ *And if any great crime or impediment be objected, the Bishop shall surcease from ordering that person, until such time as the party accused shall try himself clear of that crime.*

¶ *Then the Bishop, commending such as shall be found meet to be ordered, to the prayers of the congregation, with the Clerks, and people present, shall say or sing the Litany as followeth with the prayers.*

### THE LITANY AND SUFFRAGES.

O GOD the Father of heaven : have mercy upon us miserable sinners.
*O God the Father of heaven : have mercy upon us miserable sinners.*
O God the Son, Redeemer of the world : have mercy upon us miserable sinners.
*O God the Son, Redeemer of the world : have mercy upon us miserable sinners.*
O God the Holy Ghost, proceeding from the Father and the Son : have mercy upon us miserable sinners.
*O God the Holy Ghost, proceeding from the Father and the Son : have mercy upon us miserable sinners.*
O holy, blessed, and glorious Trinity, three Persons and one God : have mercy upon us miserable sinners.
*O holy, blessed, and glorious Trinity, three Persons and one God : have mercy upon us miserable sinners.*
Remember not, Lord, our offences, nor the offences of our forefathers, neither take thou vengeance of our sins : spare us, good Lord, spare thy people, whom thou hast redeemed with thy most precious blood, and be not angry with us for ever.
*Spare us, good Lord.*
From all evil and mischief, from sin, from the crafts and assaults of the devil, from thy wrath, and from everlasting damnation.
*Good Lord, deliver us.*

## THE ORDERING OF DEACONS. 147

From all blindness of heart, from pride, vainglory, and hypocrisy, from envy, hatred, and malice, and all uncharitableness.
*Good Lord, deliver us.*

From fornication, and all other deadly sin; and from all the deceits of the world, the flesh, and the devil.
*Good Lord, deliver us.*

From lightnings and tempests, from plague, pestilence, and famine, from battle and murther, and from sudden death.
*Good Lord, deliver us.*

From all sedition and privy conspiracy, from the tyranny of the Bishop of Rome, and all his detestable enormities, from all false doctrine and heresy, from hardness of heart, and contempt of thy word and commandment.
*Good Lord, deliver us.*

By the mystery of thy holy incarnation, by thy holy Nativity and Circumcision, by thy baptism, fasting, and temptation.
*Good Lord, deliver us.*

By thine agony and bloody sweat, by thy Cross and Passion, by thy precious death and burial, by thy glorious resurrection and ascension, and by the coming of the Holy Ghost.
*Good Lord, deliver us.*

In all time of our tribulation, in all time of our wealth, in the hour of death, and in the day of judgment.
*Good Lord, deliver us.*

We sinners do beseech thee to hear us (O Lord God), and that it may please thee to rule and govern thy holy Church universally in the right way.
*We beseech thee to hear us, good Lord.*

That it may please thee, to keep EDWARD the Sixth thy servant, our King and governor.
*We beseech thee to hear us, good Lord.*

That it may please thee, to rule his heart in thy

faith, fear and love, that he may always have affiance in thee, and ever seek thy honour and glory.
*We beseech thee to hear us, good Lord.*

That it may please thee to be his defender and keeper, giving him the victory over all his enemies.
*We beseech thee to hear us, good Lord.*

That it may please thee, to illuminate all Bishops, Pastors, and Ministers of the Church, with true knowledge, and understanding of thy word, and that both by their preaching and living they may set it forth, and shew it accordingly.
*We beseech thee to hear us, good Lord.*

That it may please thee, to bless these men, and send thy grace upon them, that they may duly execute the office, now to be committed unto them, to the edifying of thy Church, and to thy honour, praise, and glory.
*We beseech thee to hear us, good Lord.*

That it may please thee to endue the Lords of the Council, and all the nobility, with grace, wisdom, and understanding.
*We beseech thee to hear us, good Lord.*

That it may please thee, to bless and keep the Magistrates, giving them grace to execute justice, and to maintain truth.
*We beseech thee to hear us, good Lord.*

That it may please thee, to bless and keep all thy people.
*We beseech thee to hear us, good Lord.*

That it may please thee, to give to all nations unity, peace, and concord.
*We beseech thee to hear us, good Lord.*

That it may please thee, to give us an heart, to love and dread thee, and diligently to live after thy commandments.
*We beseech thee to hear us, good Lord.*

That it may please thee, to give all thy people

# THE ORDERING OF DEACONS. 149

increase of grace, to hear meekly thy word, and to receive it with pure affection, and to bring forth the fruits of the Spirit.

*We beseech thee to hear us, good Lord.*

That it may please thee, to bring into the way of truth all such as have erred and are [x] deceived.

*We beseech thee to hear us, good Lord.*

That it may please thee, to strengthen such as do stand, and to comfort and help the weak hearted, and to raise them up that fall, and finally to beat down Sathan under our feet.

*We beseech thee to hear us, good Lord.*

That it may please thee, to succour, help and comfort, all that be in danger, necessity and tribulation.

*We beseech thee to hear us, good Lord.*

That it may please thee, to preserve all that travel by land, or by water, all women labouring of child, all sick persons, and young children, and to shew thy pity upon all prisoners and captives.

*We beseech thee to hear us, good Lord.*

That it may please thee, to defend and provide for the fatherless children and widows, and all that be desolate and oppressed.

*We beseech thee to hear us, good Lord.*

That it may please thee, to have mercy upon all men.

*We beseech thee to hear us, good Lord.*

That it may please thee, to forgive our enemies, persecutors, and slanderers, and to turn their hearts.

*We beseech thee to hear us, good Lord.*

That it may please thee, to give and preserve to our use the kindly fruits of the earth, so as in due time we may enjoy them.

*We beseech thee to hear us, good Lord.*

That it may please thee, to give us true repentance, to forgive us all our sins, negligences, and ignorances,

---

[x] In some copies, "be."

and to endue us with the grace of thy holy Spirit, to amend our lives according to thy holy word.
*We beseech thee to hear us, good Lord.*

Son of God : we beseech thee to hear us.
*Son of God : we beseech thee to hear us.*

O Lamb of God, that takest away the sins of the world.
*Grant us thy peace.*

O Lamb of God, that takest away the sins of the world.
*Have mercy upon us.*

O Christ, hear us.
*O Christ, hear us.*

Lord, have mercy upon us.
*Lord, have mercy upon us.*

Christ, have mercy upon us.
*Christ, have mercy upon us.*

Lord, have mercy upon us.
*Lord, have mercy upon us.*

¶ Our Father, which art in heaven, &c.
*And lead us not into temptation.*

But deliver us from evil.

*The Versicle.* O Lord, deal not with us after our sins.

*The Answer.* Neither reward us after our iniquities.

Let us pray.

O GOD merciful Father, that despisest not the sighing of a contrite heart, nor the desire of such as be sorrowful, mercifully assist our prayers that we make before thee, in all our troubles and adversities, whensoever they oppress us : and graciously hear us, that those evils, which the craft and subtilty of the devil, or man, worketh against us, be brought to nought, and by the providence of thy goodness they may be dispersed, that we thy servants, being hurt by no persecutions, may evermore give thanks unto [7] thee, in thy holy Church : through Jesus Christ our Lord.

*O Lord, arise, help us, and deliver us, for thy name's sake.*

O GOD, we have heard with our ears, and our fathers have declared unto us, the noble works, that thou didst in their days, and in the old time before them.

*O Lord, arise, help us, and deliver us, for thine* [8] *honour.*

Glory be to the Father, and to the Son, and to the Holy Ghost. As it was in the beginning, is now, and ever shall be, world without end. Amen.

From our enemies defend us, O Christ.

*Graciously look upon our afflictions.*

Pitifully behold the sorrows of our heart.

*Mercifully forgive the sins of thy people.*

Favourably with mercy hear our prayers.

*O Son of David, have mercy upon us.*

Both now and ever vouchsafe to hear us, O Christ.

*Graciously hear us, O Christ.*

*Graciously hear us, O Lord Christ.*

*The Versicle.* O Lord, let thy mercy be shewed upon us.

*The Answer.* As we do put our trust in thee.

Let us pray.

WE humbly beseech thee, O Father, mercifully to look upon our infirmities, and for the glory of thy name's sake, turn from us all those evils, that we most righteously have deserved : And grant that in all our troubles we may put our whole trust and confidence in thy mercy, and evermore serve thee, in holiness and pureness of living, to thy honour and glory, through our only mediator and advocate Jesus Christ our Lord. Amen.

ALMIGHTY God, which hast given us grace at this

---

[7] In some copies, "to thee."   [8] In some copies, "*thy*."

time with one accord to make our common supplications unto thee, and dost promise, that when two or three be gathered in thy name, thou wilt grant their requests: fulfil now, O Lord, the desires and petitions of thy servants, as may be most expedient for them, granting us in this world knowledge of thy truth, and in the world to come life everlasting. Amen.

*Then shall be said also this that followeth.*

ALMIGHTY God, which by thy divine providence hast appointed diverse Orders of ministers in the Church, and didst inspire thine holy Apostles to choose unto this Order of Deacons the first Martyr saint Stephin, with other: mercifully behold these thy servants, now called to the like office and administration; replenish them so with the truth of thy doctrine, and innocency of life, that, both by word and good example, they may faithfully serve thee in this office, to the glory of thy name, and profit of the congregation, through the merits of our Saviour Jesu Christ, who liveth and reigneth with thee, and the Holy Ghost, now and ever. Amen.

*Then shall be sung or said, the Communion of the day, saving the Epistle shall be read out of Timothy, as followeth.*

LIKEWISE must the ministers be honest, not double-tongued, nor given unto much wine, neither greedy of filthy lucre, but holding the mystery of the faith, with a pure conscience. And let them first be proved, and then let them minister so that no man be able to reprove them. Even so must their wives be honest, not evil speakers, but sober, and faithful in all things. Let the Deacons be the husbands of one wife, and such as rule their children well, and their own households. For they that minister well get themselves a good degree, and a great liberty in the faith which is in Christ Jesu.

These things write I unto thee trusting to come shortly unto thee; but and if I tarry long, that then

# THE ORDERING OF DEACONS. 153

thou mayest yet have knowledge, how thou oughtest to behave thyself in the house of God, which is the congregation of the living God, the pillar and ground of truth. And without doubt great is that mystery of godliness. God was shewed in the flesh, was justified in the spirit, was seen among the angels, was preached unto the Gentiles, was believed on in the world, and received up in glory.

*Or else this, out of the sixth of the Acts.*

THEN the twelve called the multitude of the disciples together, and said : It is not meet that we should leave the Word of God, and serve tables. Wherefore, brethren, look ye out among you seven men of honest report, and full of the holy Ghost and wisdom, to whom we may commit this business. But we will give ourselves continually to prayer, and to the administration of the Word. And that saying pleased the whole multitude. And they chose Stephen, a man full of faith, and full of the holy Ghost, and Philip, and Prochorus, and Nicanor, and Timon, and Permenas, and Nicolas a convert of Antioch. These they set before the Apostles : and, when they had prayed, they laid their hands on them. And the Word of God increased, and the number of the disciples multiplied in Jerusalem greatly, and a great company of the Priests, were obedient unto the faith.

¶ *And before the Gospel, the Bishop sitting in a Chair, shall cause the Oath of the King's Supremacy, and*[a] *against the usurped power and authority of the Bishop of Rome, to be ministered unto every of them, that are to be ordered.*

¶ *The Oath of the King's Supremacy.*

I FROM henceforth shall utterly renounce, refuse, relinquish, and forsake the Bishop of Rome, and his authority, power, and jurisdiction. And I shall never

---
[a] In some copies, "and" *omitted.*

consent nor agree, that the bishop of Rome shall practise, exercise, or have, any manner of authority, jurisdiction, or power within this realm, or any other the King's dominions, but shall resist the same at all times, to the uttermost of my power. And I from henceforth will accept, repute, and take the King's Majesty to be the only Supreme head in earth, of the Church of England: And to my cunning, wit, and uttermost of my power, without guile, fraud, or other undue mean, I will observe, keep, maintain and defend, the whole effects and contents of all and singular acts and Statutes made, and to be made within this realm, in derogation, extirpation, and extinguishment of the Bishop [b] of Rome, and his authority, and all other Acts and Statutes, made or to be made, in confirmation and corroboration of the King's power, of the supreme head in earth, of the Church of England: and this I will do against all manner of persons, of what estate, dignity or degree, or condition they be, and in no wise do nor attempt, nor to my power suffer to be done or attempted, directly, or indirectly, any thing or things, privily or apertly, to the let, hinderance, damage, or derogation thereof, or any part thereof, by any manner of means, or for any manner of pretence. And in case any oath be made, or hath been made, by me, to any person or persons, in maintenance, defence, or favour of the Bishop of Rome, or his authority, jurisdiction, or power, I repute the same as vain and annihilate, so help me God through Jesus Christ.

¶ *Then shall the Bishop examine every one of them, that are to be ordered, in the presence of the people, after this manner following.*

Do you trust that you are inwardly moved by the Holy Ghost to take upon you this office and minis-

---

[b] In some copies, "B. of Rome."

tration, to serve God, for the promoting of his glory, and the edifying of his people?

*Answer.* I trust so.

*The Bishop.* Do ye think, that ye truly be called, according to the will of our Lord Jesus Christ, and the due order of this realm to the ministry of the church?

*Answer.* I think so.

*The Bishop.* Do ye unfeignedly believe all the Canonical scriptures, of the old and new Testament?

*Answer.* I do believe.

*The Bishop.* Will you diligently read the same unto the people assembled in the Church where you shall be appointed to serve?

*Answer.* I will.

*The Bishop.* It pertaineth to the office of a Deacon in the Church where he shall be appointed to assist the Priest in divine service, and specially when he ministereth the holy Communion, and to help him in distribution thereof, and to read holy scriptures and Homilies in the congregation, and to instruct the youth in the Catechism, to baptize and to preach if he be admitted thereto by the Bishop. And furthermore, it is his office where provision is so made to search for the sick, poor, and impotent people of the parish, and to intimate their estates, names, and places where they dwell to the Curate, that by his exhortation they may be relieved by the parish or other convenient alms: will you do this gladly and willingly?

*Answer.* I will so do by the help of God.

*The Bishop.* Will you apply all your diligence to frame and fashion your own lives, and the lives of all your family according to the doctrine of Christ, and to make both yourselves and them, as much as in you lieth, wholesome examples of the flock of Christ?

*Answer.* I will so do, the Lord being my helper.

*The Bishop.* Will you reverently obey your ordinary, and other chief Ministers of the Church, and them to whom the government and charge is committed over you, following with a glad mind and will their godly admonitions?

*Answer.* I will thus endeavour myself, the Lord being my helper.

¶ *Then the Bishop laying his hands severally upon the head of every of them, shall say.*

Take thou authority to execute the office of a Deacon in the Church of God committed unto thee: in the name of the Father, the Son, and the Holy Ghost. Amen.

*Then shall the Bishop deliver to every one of them the new Testament, saying.*

Take thou authority to read the Gospel in the Church of God, and to preach the same, if thou be thereunto ordinarily commanded.

*Then one of them, appointed by the Bishop, shall read the Gospel of that day.*

*Then shall the Bishop proceed to the Communion, and all that be ordered, shall tarry and receive the holy Communion the same day with the Bishop.*

*The Communion ended, after the last Collect and immediately before the benediction, shall be said this Collect following.*

ALMIGHTY God, giver of all good things, which of thy great goodness hast vouchsafed to accept and take these thy servants unto the office of Deacons in thy Church: make them, we beseech thee, O Lord, to be modest, humble, and constant in their ministration, to have a ready will to observe all spiritual discipline, that they having always the testimony of a good conscience, and continuing ever stable and strong in thy Son Christ, may so well use themselves in this inferior office, that they may be found worthy to be called unto the higher ministries in thy Church, through the same thy Son our Saviour Christ, to whom be glory and honour world without end. Amen.

¶ *And here it must be shewed unto the Deacon, that he must continue in that office of a Deacon the space of a <sup>c</sup> whole year at the least (except for reasonable causes it be otherwise seen to his Ordinary) to the intent he may be perfect, and well expert in the things appertaining to the Ecclesiastical administration, in executing whereof if he be found faithful and diligent, he may be admitted by his Diocesan to the order of Priesthood.*

<sup>c</sup> In some copies, "an."

¶ THE FORM

OF

ORDERING PRIESTS.

*When the exhortation is ended, then shall follow the Communion. And for the Epistle shall be read out of the twentieth Chapter of the Acts of the Apostles as followeth.*

FROM Mileto Paul sent messengers to Ephesus, and called the elders of the congregation, which when they were come to him, he said unto them, Ye know, that from the first day that I came into Asia, after what manner I have been with you at all seasons, serving the Lord with all humbleness of mind, and with many tears and temptations which happened unto me by the layings await of the Jews; because I would keep back nothing that was profitable unto you, but to shew you, and teach you openly throughout every house: witnessing both to the Jews, and also to the Greeks, the repentance that is towards God, and the faith which is toward our Lord Jesus Christ. And now behold, I go bound in the spirit unto Jerusalem, not knowing the things that shall come on me there; but that the Holy Ghost witnesseth in every city, saying, that bonds and trouble abide me. But none of these things move me, neither is my life dear unto myself, that I might fulfil my course with joy, and the ministration of the word which I have received of the Lord Jesu, to testify the Gospel of the grace of God. And now behold, I am sure that henceforth ye all, through whom I have gone preaching the kingdom of God, shall see my face no more. Wherefore I take you to record this day, that I am pure from the blood of all men. For I have spared no labour, but have shewed you all the counsel of God. Take heed therefore unto yourselves, and to all the flock amongst whom the Holy Ghost hath made you Overseers, to rule the congregation of God, which he hath purchased with his blood. For I am sure of this, that after my departing shall grievous wolves enter in among you, not sparing the flock. Moreover of your own selves shall men arise speaking perverse things, to draw disciples after them. Therefore awake and remember, that by the space of three years, I ceased not to warn every one of you night and day with tears. And now, brethren, I commend you to God, and to the word of his grace, which is able to build further, and to give you an inheritance among all them which are sanctified. I have desired no man's silver, gold, or vesture; Yea, you know yourselves, that these hands have ministered unto my necessities, and to them that were with me. I have shewed you all things, how that so labouring ye ought to receive the weak; and to remember the words of the Lord Jesu, how that he said, It is more blessed to give than to receive.

*Or else this third Chapter of the first Epistle to Timothy.*

THIS is a true saying, If any man desire the Office of a Bishop, he desireth an honest work. A Bishop therefore must be blameless, the husband of one wife, vigilant, sober, discreet, a keeper of hospitality, apt to teach; not given to overmuch wine, no fighter, not greedy of filthy lucre, but gentle, abhorring fighting, abhorring covetousness; one that ruleth well his own house, one that hath children in subjection with all reverence. (For if a man cannot rule his own house, how shall he care for the congregation of God?) He may not be a young scholar, lest he swell and fall into the judgement of the evil speaker. He must also have a good report of them which are without; lest he fall into rebuke and snare of the evil speaker.

Likewise must the ministers be honest, not double-tongued, not given unto much wine, neither greedy of filthy lucre; but holding the mystery of the faith with a pure conscience; and let them first be proved, and then let them minister so that no man be able to reprove them.

Even so must their wives be honest; not evil-speakers, but sober and faithful in all things. Let the deacons be the husbands of one wife, and such as rule their children well and their own households, for they that minister well get themselves a good degree and great liberty in the faith which is in Christ Jesu.

These things write I unto thee, trusting to come shortly unto thee, but, and if I tarry long, that then thou mayest have yet knowledge how thou oughtest to behave thy self in the house of God, which is the congregation of the living God, the Pillar and ground of truth. And without doubt, great is that mystery of Godliness. God was shewed in the flesh, was Justified in the Spirit, was seen among the Angels, was preached unto the Gentiles, was believed on in the world, and received up in glory.

*After this shall be read for the Gospel a piece of the last Chapter of Matthew, as followeth.*

JESUS came and spake unto them, saying: All power is given unto me in heaven and in earth. Go ye therefore and teach all nations, baptizing them In the name of the father, and of the son, and of the holy ghost. Teaching them to observe all things, whatsoever I have commanded you. And lo, I am with you alway, even until the end of the world.

*Or else this that followeth, of the x. Chapter of John.*

VERILY, verily I say unto you, He that entereth not in by the door into the sheep-fold, but climbeth up some other way, the same is a thief and a murtherer. But he that entereth in by the door is the

Shepherd of the sheep. To him the porter openeth, and the sheep heareth his voice, and he calleth his own sheep by name, and leadeth them out. And when he hath sent forth his own sheep he goeth before them, and the sheep follow him, for they know his voice. A stranger will they not follow, but will flee from him; for they know not the voice of strangers. This Proverb spake Jesus unto them, but they understood not what things they were which he spake unto them. Then said Jesus unto them again, Verily, verily I say unto you, I am the door of the sheep. All (even as many as come before me) are thieves and murtherers: but the sheep did not hear them. I am the door, by me if any man enter in, he shall be safe, and go in and out, and find pasture. A thief cometh not but for to steal, kill, and to destroy. I am come that they might have life, and that they might have it more abundantly. I am the good Shepherd: a good Shepherd giveth his life for the sheep. An hired servant, and he which is not the Shepherd (neither the sheep are his own) seeth the wolf coming, and leaveth the sheep, and fleeth, and the wolf catcheth and scattereth the sheep. The hired servant fleeth, because he is an hired servant, and careth not for the sheep. I am the good Shepherd and know my sheep, and am known of mine. As my Father knoweth me, even so know I also my Father. And I give my life for the sheep. And other sheep I have, which are not of this fold. Them also must I bring, and they shall hear my voice, and there shall be one fold, and one Shepherd.

*Or else this, of the xx. chapter of John.*

THE same day at night, which was the first day of the Sabboths, when the doors were shut (where the disciples were assembled together for fear of the Jews) came Jesus and stood in the midst, and saith unto them, Peace be unto you. And when he had so said, he shewed unto them his hands and his side. Then were the disciples glad, when they saw the Lord. Then said Jesus unto them again, Peace be unto you. As my Father sent me, even so send I you also. And when he had said these words, he breathed on them, and said unto them, Receive ye the holy ghost: whosoever sins ye remit, they are remitted unto them: and whosoever sins ye retain, they are retained.

*When the Gospel is ended, then shall be said or sung.*

COME, Holy Ghost, eternal God, proceeding from above,
Both from the Father and the Son, the God of peace and love:
Visit our minds, and into us thy heavenly grace inspire,
That in all truth and godliness we may have true desire.
Thou art the very Comforter, in all woe and distress,
The heavenly gift of God most high, which no tongue can express,
The fountain and the lively spring of joy celestial,
The fire so bright, the love so clear, and Unction spiritual.
Thou in thy gifts art manifold, whereby Christ's Church doth stand,
In faithful hearts writing thy [d] law, the finger of God's hand:
According to thy promise made, thou givest speech of grace,
That through thy help, the praise of God may sound in every place.

[d] In some copies, "the law."

O Holy Ghost, into our wits send down thy heavenly light,
Kindle our hearts with fervent love, to serve God day and night,
Strength and stablish all our weakness, so feeble and so frail,
That neither flesh, the world, nor devil, against us do prevail.
Put back our enemy far from us, and grant us to obtain
Peace in our hearts with God and man, without grudge or disdain.
And grant, O Lord, that thou being our leader and our guide,
We may eschew the snares of sin, and from thee never slide.
To us such plenty of thy grace, good Lord, grant, we thee pray,
That thou Lord mayest be our comfort\*, at the last dreadful day.
Of all strife and dissension, O Lord, dissolve the bands,
And make the knots of peace and love throughout all Christian lands.
Grant us, O Lord, through thee to know the Father most of might,
That of his dear beloved Son we may attain the sight:
And that with perfect faith also we may acknowledge thee,
The Spirit of them both, alway one God in persons three.

\* In some copies, "That thou mayest be our Comforter."

Laud and praise be to the Father, and to the Son equal,

And to the Holy Spirit also, one God coeternal:

And pray we that the only Son vouchsafe his Spirit to send

To all that do profess his name, unto the world's end. Amen.

*And then the Archdeacon shall present unto the Bishop all them that shall receive the order of Priesthood that day. The Archdeacon saying.*

REVEREND father in God, I present unto you these persons present, to be admitted to the Order of Priesthood, *Cum interrogatione et responsione, ut in Ordine Diaconatus.*

*And then the Bishop shall say to the people.*

GOOD people, these be they whom we purpose, God willing, to receive this day unto the holy office of Priesthood. For after due examination, we find not the contrary, but that they be lawfully called to their function and ministry, and that they be persons meet for the same: but yet if there be any of you, which knoweth any impediment, or notable crime in any of them, for the which he ought not to be received into this holy ministry, now in the name of God declare the same.

¶ *And if any great crime or impediment be objected, &c.* Ut supra in Ordine Diaconatus usque ad finem Litaniæ cum hac Collecta.

ALMIGHTY GOD, giver of all good things, which by thy Holy Spirit hast appointed diverse orders of Ministers in thy church: mercifully behold these thy servants, now called to the office of Priesthood, and replenish them so with the truth of thy doctrine, and innocency of life, that both by word and good example they may faithfully serve thee in this office, to the glory of thy name, and profit of the congregation, through the merits of our Saviour Jesu Christ, who liveth and reigneth, with thee and the Holy Ghost, world without end. Amen.

*Then the Bishop shall minister unto every of them the oath, concerning the King's Supremacy, as it is set out in the Order of Deacons. And that done, he shall say unto them, which are appointed to receive the said office, as hereafter followeth.*

YOU have heard, brethren, as well in your private examination, as in the exhortation, and in the holy lessons taken out of the Gospel, and of the writings of the Apostles, of what dignity, and of how great importance this office is, (whereunto ye be called). And now we exhort you, in the name of our Lord Jesus Christ, to have in remembrance, into how high a dignity, and to how chargeable an office ye be called, that is to say, to be the messengers, the watchmen, the Pastors, and the stewards of the Lord, to teach, to premonish, to feed, and provide for the Lord's family: to seek for Christ's Sheep, that be dispersed abroad, and for his children, which be in the midst of this naughty world, to be saved through Christ for ever. Have always therefore printed in your remembrance, how great a treasure is committed to your charge: for they be the Sheep of Christ, which he bought with his death, and for whom he shed his blood. The Church and congregation, whom you must serve, is his spouse and his body. And if it shall chance the same Church, or any member thereof, to take any hurt or hinderance by reason of your negligence, ye know the greatness of the fault, and also of the horrible punishment which will ensue. Wherefore, consider with yourselves the end of your ministry, towards the children of God, toward the spouse and body of Christ, and see that ye never cease your labour, your care and diligence, until you have done all that lieth in you, according to your bounden duty, to bring all such as are, or shall be committed to your charge, unto that agreement in faith, and knowledge of God, and to that ripeness, and perfectness of age in Christ, that there be no place left among them, either for error in religion, or for viciousness in life.

Then forasmuch as your office is both of so great excellency, and of so great difficulty, ye see with how great care and study ye ought to apply yourselves, as well that you may shew yourselves kind to that Lord, who hath placed you in so high a dignity, as also to beware, that neither you yourselves offend, neither be occasion that other offend. Howbeit ye cannot have a mind and a will thereto of yourselves, for that power and ability is given of God alone. Therefore ye see how ye ought and have need, earnestly to pray for his Holy Spirit. And seeing that you cannot, by any other means, compass the doing of so weighty a work, pertaining to the salvation of man, but with doctrine and exhortation, taken out of holy Scripture, and with a life agreeable unto the same, ye perceive how studious ye ought to be in reading and in learning the holy scriptures, and in framing the manners, both of yourselves, and of them that specially pertain unto you, according to the rule of the same scriptures. And for this self same cause, ye see how you ought to forsake and set aside (as much as you may) all worldly cares and studies.

We have a good hope, that you have well weighed and pondered these things with yourselves, long before this time, and that you have clearly determined, by God's grace, to give yourselves wholly to this vocation, whereunto it hath pleased God to call you, so that (as much as lieth in you) you apply yourselves wholly to this one thing, and draw all your cares and studies this way, and to this end. And that you will continually pray for the heavenly assistance of the Holy Ghost, from God the Father, by the mediation of our only Mediator and Saviour Jesus Christ, that by daily reading and weighing of the scriptures ye may wax riper and stronger in your Ministry. And that ye [f] may so endeavour yourselves, from time to time, to sanctify the lives of you and yours, and to fashion them, after the rule and doctrine of Christ, and that ye may be wholesome and godly examples and patterns, for the rest of the congregation to follow:

And that this present congregation of Christ, here assembled, may also understand your minds and wills, in these things: and that this your promise shall more move you to do your duties, ye shall answer plainly to these things, which we in the name of the Congregation shall demand of you, touching the same.

Do you think in your heart, that you be truly called, according to the will of our Lord Jesus Christ, and the order of this Church of England, to the ministry of Priesthood?

*Answer.* I think it.

*The Bishop.* Be you persuaded that the holy scriptures contain sufficiently all doctrine, required of necessity for eternal salvation, through faith in Jesu Christ? And are you determined with the said scriptures to instruct the people committed to your charge, and to teach nothing, (as required of necessity to eternal salvation,) but that you shall be persuaded, may be concluded, and proved by the scripture?

*Answer.* I am so persuaded, and have so determined by God's grace.

*The Bishop.* Will you then give your faithful diligence always, so to minister the doctrine, and Sacraments, and the discipline of Christ, as the Lord hath commanded, and as this realm hath received the same, according to the commandments of God, so that you may teach the people committed to your

[f] In some copies, "you."

cure and charge with all diligence to keep and observe the same?

*Answer.* I will so do, by the help of the Lord.

*The Bishop.* Will you be ready with all faithful diligence to banish and drive away all erroneous and strange doctrines, contrary to God's word, and to use both public and private monitions and exhortations, as well to the sick as to the whole, within your cures, as need shall require and occasion be given?

*Answer.* I will, the Lord being my helper.

*The Bishop.* Will you be diligent in prayers and in reading of the holy scriptures, and in such studies as help to the knowledge of the same, laying aside the study of the world and the flesh?

*Answer.* I will endeavour myself so to do, the Lord being my helper.

*The Bishop.* Will you be diligent to frame and fashion your own selves and your families according to the doctrine of Christ, and to make both yourselves and them (as much as in you lieth) wholesome examples and spectacles to the flock of Christ?

*Answer.* I will so apply myself, the Lord being my helper.

*The Bishop.* Will you maintain and set forwards (as much as lieth in you) quietness, peace, and love amongst all christian people, and specially amongst[s] them that are or shall be committed to your charge?

*Answer.* I will so do, the Lord being my helper.

*The Bishop.* Will you reverently obey your ordinary, and other chief ministers, unto whom the government and charge is committed over you, following with a glad mind and will their godly admonition, and submitting yourselves to their godly judgments?

*Answer.* I will so do, the Lord being my helper.

*Then shall the Bishop say,*

ALMIGHTY God, who hath given you this will to

---

[s] In some copies, "among."

# THE ORDERING OF PRIESTS.

do all these things, grant also unto you strength and power to perform the same, that he may accomplish his work which he hath begun in you, until the time he shall come at the latter day to judge the quick and the dead.

*After this the congregation shall be desired secretly in their prayers to make humble supplications to God for the foresaid things, for the which prayers there shall be a certain space kept in silence.*

*That done, the Bishop shall pray in this wise.*

¶ Let us pray.

ALMIGHTY God and heavenly Father, which of thy infinite love and goodness towards us, hast given to us thy only and most dear beloved Son Jesus Christ, to be our redeemer and author of everlasting life: who after he had made perfect our redemption by his death, and was ascended into heaven, sent abroad into the world his Apostles, Prophets, Evangelists, Doctors, and Pastors, by whose labour and ministry he gathered together a great flock in all the parts of the world, to set forth the eternal praise of thy holy name: For these so great benefits of thy eternal goodness, and for that thou hast vouchsafed to call these thy servants here present to the same office and ministry of the salvation of mankind, we render unto thee most hearty thanks, we worship and praise thee; and we humbly beseech thee by the same thy Son, to grant unto all us which either here or elsewhere call upon thy name, that we may shew ourselves thankful to thee for these and all other thy[h] benefits, and that we may daily increase and go forwards in the knowledge and faith of thee, and thy Son, by the Holy Spirit. So that as well by these thy ministers, as by them to whom they shall be appointed ministers, thy

---

[h] In some copies, "the."

holy name may be always glorified, and thy blessed kingdom enlarged: through the same thy Son our Lord Jesus Christ: which liveth and reigneth with thee in the unity of the same Holy Spirit world without end. Amen.

¶ *When this prayer is done, the Bishop with the Priests present shall lay their hands severally upon the head of every one that receiveth orders: the receivers humbly kneeling upon their knees, and the Bishop saying:*

RECEIVE the Holy Ghost: whose sins thou dost forgive, they are forgiven: and whose sins thou dost retain, they are retained: and be thou a faithful dispenser of the word of God, and of his holy sacraments. In the name of the Father, and of the Son, and of the Holy Ghost. Amen.

¶ *The Bishop shall deliver to every one of them the Bible in his hand, saying.*

TAKE thou authority to preach the word of God, and to minister the holy Sacraments in this congregation where thou shalt be so appointed.

¶ *When this is done, the congregation shall sing the Creed, and also they shall go to the Communion, which all they that receive orders shall take together, and remain in the same place where the hands were laid upon them, until such time as they have received the Communion.*

¶ *The Communion being done, after the last Collect, and immediately before the benediction, shall be said this Collect.*

MOST merciful Father, we beseech thee, so to send upon these thy servants thy heavenly blessing, that they may be clad about with all justice, and that thy word spoken by their mouths may have such success, that it may never be spoken in vain. Grant also that we may have grace to hear and receive the same as thy most holy word and the mean of our salvation, that in all our words and deeds we may seek thy glory and the increase of thy kingdom, through Jesus Christ our Lord. Amen.

¶ *And if the Orders of Deacon and Priesthood be given both upon one day, then shall all things at the holy Communion be used as they are appointed at the ordering of Priests. Saving that for the Epistle, the whole third chapter of the first to Timothy shall be read, as it is set out before in the order of Priests. And immediately after the Epistle, the Deacons shall be ordered. And it shall suffice the Litany to be said once.*

# THE FORM OF CONSECRATING

## OF AN

## ARCHBISHOP OR BISHOP

¶ *At the Communion*[1].

### *The Epistle.*

THIS is a true saying, If a man desire the office of a Bishop, he desireth an honest work. A Bishop therefore must be blameless, the husband of one wife, diligent, sober, discreet, a keeper of hospitality, apt to teach, not given to overmuch wine, no fighter, not greedy of filthy lucre, but gentle, abhorring fighting, abhorring covetousness, one that ruleth well his own house; one that hath children in subjection with all reverence. For if a man cannot rule his own house, how shall he care for the congregation of God? he may not be a young scholar, lest he swell, and fall into the judgment of the evil speaker. He must also have a good report of them which are without, lest he fall into rebuke and snare of the evil speaker. 1 Tim. iii.

### *The Gospel.*

JESUS said to Simon Peter, Simon Johanna, lovest thou me more than these? He said unto him, Yea, Lord, thou knowest that I love thee. He said unto him, Feed my lambs. He said to him again the second time: Simon Johanna, lovest thou me? He said unto him, Yea, Lord, thou knowest that I love thee. He said unto him, Feed my sheep. He said unto him the third time, Simon Johanna, lovest thou me? Peter was sorry because he said unto him the third time, Lovest thou me? and he said unto him: Lord, thou knowest all things, John xxi.[k]

---

[1] In some copies, "The Epistle at the Communion." [k] In some copies, *misp.* " iiij."

thou knowest that I love thee. Jesus said unto him, Feed my sheep.

*¶ Or else out of the tenth Chapter of John, as before in the order of Priests.*

*¶ After the Gospel and* Credo *ended, first the elected Bishop, shall be presented by two Bishops unto the Archbishop of that Province, or to some other Bishop appointed by his commission: the Bishops that present him saying:*

MOST reverend father in God, we present unto you this godly and well learned man to be consecrated Bishop.

*¶ Then shall the Archbishop demand the King's mandate for the consecration, and cause it to be read. And the oath touching the knowledge of the King's supremacy shall be ministered to the person elected, as it is set out in the order of Deacons. And then shall be ministered also the Oath of due obedience unto the Archbishop as followeth.*

## ¶ THE OATH OF DUE OBEdience to the Archbishop.

IN the name of GOD, Amen. I, *N.* chosen Bishop of the church and see of *N.* do profess and promise all due reverence and obedience to the Archbishop and to the Metropolitical church of *N.* and to their successors, so help me God through Jesus Christ.

*¶ This oath shall not be made at the consecration of an Archbishop.*

*¶ Then the Archbishop shall move the congregation present to pray, saying thus to them.*

BRETHREN, it is written in the Gospel of Saint Luke, that our Saviour Christ continued the whole night in prayer or ever that he did choose and send forth his twelve Apostles. It is written also in the Acts of the Apostles, that the disciples which were at Antioch did fast and pray or ever they laid hands upon or sent forth Paul and Barnabas. Let us therefore, following the example of our Saviour Christ and his Apostles, first fall to prayer or that we admit and send forth this person presented unto us, to the work whereunto we trust the Holy Ghost hath called him.

¶ *And then shall be said the Litany as afore in the order of Deacons. And after this place: That it may please thee to illuminate all Bishops &c. he shall say.*

THAT it may please thee to bless this our brother elected, and to send thy grace upon him, that he may duly execute the office whereunto he is called, to the edifying of thy church, and to the honour, praise and glory of thy name.

*Answer.* We beseech thee to hear us, good Lord.

¶ *Concluding the Litany in the end with this prayer:*

ALMIGHTY God, giver of all good things, which by thy Holy Spirit hast appointed divers orders of Ministers in thy Church: mercifully behold this thy servant now called to the work and ministry of a Bishop, and replenish him so with the truth of thy doctrine and innocency of life, that both by word and deed he may faithfully serve thee in this office, to the glory of thy name, and profit of thy congregation : Through the merits of our Saviour Jesu Christ, who liveth and reigneth with thee and the Holy Ghost, world without end. Amen.

¶ *Then the Archbishop sitting in a chair, shall say this to him that is to be consecrated.*

BROTHER, forasmuch as holy Scripture and the old Canons commandeth that we should not be hasty in laying on hands and admitting of any person to the government of the congregation of Christ, which he hath purchased with no less price than the effusion of his own blood : afore that I admit you to this administration whereunto ye are called, I will examine

# CONSECRATION OF BISHOPS. 175

you in certain articles, to the end the congregation present may have a trial and bear witness how ye be minded to behave yourself in the church of God. Are you persuaded that you be truly called to this ministration according to the will of our Lord Jesus Christ and the order of this realm?

*Answer.* I am so persuaded.

*The Archbishop.* Are you persuaded that the holy Scriptures contain sufficiently all doctrine required of necessity for eternal salvation through the faith in Jesu Christ? And are you determined with the same holy Scriptures to instruct the people committed to your charge, and to teach or maintain nothing, as required of necessity to eternal salvation, but that you shall be persuaded may be concluded and proved by the same?

*Answer.* I am so persuaded and determined by God's grace.

*The Archbishop.* Will you then faithfully exercise yourself in the said holy Scriptures, and call upon God by prayer for the true understanding of the same, so as ye may be able by them to teach and exhort with wholesome doctrine, and to withstand and convince the gainsayers?

*Answer.* I will so do, by the help of God.

*The Archbishop.* Be you ready with all faithful diligence to banish and drive away all erroneous and strange doctrine contrary to God's word, and both privately and openly to call upon, and encourage other to the same?

*Answer.* I am ready, the Lord being my helper.

*The Archbishop.* Will you deny all ungodliness, and worldly lusts, and live soberly, righteously, and godly in this world, that you may shew yourself in all things an example of good works unto other, that the adversary may be ashamed, having nothing to lay against you?

*Answer.* I will so do, the Lord being my helper.

*The Archbishop.* Will you maintain and set forward (as much as shall lie in you) quietness, peace, and love, among all men? And such as be unquiet, disobedient, and criminous within your diocese, correct and punish, according to such authority, as ye have by God's word, and as to you shall be committed, by the ordinance of this realm?

*Answer.* I will so do, by the help of God.

*The Archbishop.* Will you shew yourself gentle, and be merciful for Christ's sake, to poor and needy people, and to all strangers destitute of help?

*Answer.* I will so shew myself by God's help.

*The Archbishop.* Almighty God our heavenly Father, who hath given you a good will to do all these things: grant also unto you strength and power, to perform the same, that he accomplishing in you the good work which he hath begun, ye may be found perfect, and irreprehensible at the latter day: through Jesu Christ our Lord. Amen.

*Then shall be sung or said,* Come Holy Ghost, *&c. as it is set out in the Order of Priests.*

*That ended, the Archbishop shall say,*

Lord, hear our prayer.
*Answer.* And let our cry come unto thee.

¶ Let us pray.

ALMIGHTY God and most merciful Father, which of thy infinite goodness, hast given to us thy only and most dear beloved Son Jesus Christ, to be our redeemer and author of everlasting life, who after that he had made perfect our redemption by his death, and was ascended into heaven, poured down his gifts abundantly upon men, making some Apostles, some Prophets, some Evangelists, some Pastors and Doctors, to the edifying and making perfect of his congregation: Grant, we beseech thee, to this thy servant such grace, that he may evermore be ready to spread abroad thy Gospel, and glad tidings of reconcilement to God, and to use the authority given unto him, not to destroy, but to save, not to hurt, but to help, so that he as a wise and a faithful servant, giving to thy family meat in due season, may at the last day be received into joy, through Jesu Christ our Lord, who with thee and the Holy Ghost liveth and reigneth one God, world without end. Amen.

¶ *Then the Archbishop and Bishops present shall lay their hands upon the head of the elected Bishop, the Archbishop saying.*

TAKE the Holy Ghost, and remember that thou stir up the grace of God, which is in thee, by imposition of hands: for God hath not given us the spirit of fear, but of power, and love, and of soberness.

¶ *Then the Archbishop shall deliver him the Bible, saying.*

GIVE heed unto reading, exhortation and doctrine. Think upon these things contained in this book, be diligent in them, that the increase[1] coming thereby may be manifest unto all men. Take heed unto thyself, and unto teaching, and be diligent in doing them: for by doing this thou shalt save thyself and them that hear thee; be to the flock of Christ a shepherd, not a wolf, feed them, devour them not, hold up the weak, heal the sick, bind together the broken, bring again the outcasts, seek the lost: Be so merciful, that you be not too remiss, so minister discipline, that you forget not mercy: that when the chief Shepherd shall come, ye may receive the immarcessible crown of glory, through Jesus Christ our Lord. Amen.

¶ *Then the Archbishop shall proceed to the Communion, with whom the new consecrated Bishop with other shall also*

---

[1] In some copies, "increasing."

*communicate. And after the last Collect, immediately before the benediction, shall be said this prayer:*

MOST merciful Father, we beseech thee to send down upon this thy servant thy heavenly blessing, and so endue him with thy Holy Spirit, that he preaching thy word, may not only be earnest to reprove, beseech, and rebuke with all patience and doctrine, but also may be to such as believe an wholesome example in word, in conversation, in love, in faith, in chastity, and purity: that faithfully fulfilling his course, at the latter day he may receive the crown of righteousness, laid up by the Lord, the righteous Judge: who liveth and reigneth, one God with the Father and the Holy Ghost, world without end. Amen.

www.ingramcontent.com/pod-product-compliance
Lightning Source LLC
Chambersburg PA
CBHW070922180426
43192CB00037B/1708